THE JEWISH HOME

THE
JEWISH HOME

A Guide for Jewish Living

◆ ◆ ◆

DANIEL B. SYME

UAHC Press · New York, New York

*Part of the greatness of Reform Judaism lies in the fact that each Jew is
free to select and observe those rituals which are most meaningful on a
personal level. But choice implies knowledge of the options available to us.
Hence this series, which will briefly present a number of these options.*

Library of Congress Cataloging-in-Publication Data

Syme, Daniel B.
The Jewish home: a guide for Jewish living/Daniel B. Syme.
p. cm.
ISBN 0-8074-0400-4
1. Judaism—Customs and practices. 2. Reform Judaism—Customs
and practices. I. Title.
BM700.S87   1988   88-14387
296.7'4—dc19   CIP

Copyright © 1988 by the UAHC Press
Manufactured in the United States of America
9 10

Feldman Library

THE FELDMAN LIBRARY FUND was created in 1974 through a gift from the Milton and Sally Feldman Foundation. The Feldman Library Fund, which provides for the publication by the UAHC of selected outstanding Jewish books and texts, memorializes Sally Feldman, who in her lifetime devoted herself to Jewish youth and Jewish learning. Herself an orphan and brought up in an orphanage, she dedicated her efforts to helping Jewish young people get the educational opportunities she had not enjoyed.

In loving memory of my beloved wife Sally
"She was my life, and she is gone;
She was my riches, and I am a pauper."

"Many daughters have done valiantly,
but thou excellest them all."

Milton E. Feldman

With profound gratitude and thanks, I dedicate this book to:

Albert Vorspan
> my friend and mentor, who first urged me to write books, and who has blessed my life with his caring.

Rabbi Bernard Zlotowitz
> my teacher and scholarly advisor, who was my strong right arm and support always.

But above all, I offer this book as a gift of love to my family:

Deborah Shayne Syme—my wife and friend, who has made our home a place of Jewish joy and celebration.

Rabbi M. Robert and Sonia Syme—my parents, who first showed me what a truly Jewish home can be.

David Syme and Michael Syme ז"ל —my brothers, with whom I shared the holidays and the festivals, and a sense of wonder at the beauty of Judaism.

and

Joshua Shayne Syme—my son, my treasure, through whose eyes I see the future and through whose Jewish identity I know it is secure.

Acknowledgments

The "Jewish Home" series in *Reform Judaism* magazine came into being in 1974 at the suggestion of Albert Vorspan, senior vice president of the UAHC. Over the ensuing thirteen years, dozens of friends generously helped to shape the contents of this book, far too many to mention each by name. There are some, however, who must be singled out for special thanks.

Aron Hirt-Manheimer, Joy Weinberg, and the staff of *Reform Judaism* kept the series on deadline and on track. Stuart L. Benick, UAHC director of Publications, oversaw the production of each "Jewish Home" booklet and this single volume with his rare genius. Josette Knight and Annette Abramson meticulously copyedited each of the more than sixty articles, selected photographs that sensitively reflected the tone of each piece in turn, and made countless wise editorial suggestions.

Close to one hundred colleagues read one or more of the individual articles. I wish to thank them all, but particularly Rabbi Bernard Zlotowitz, who served as chief scholarly advisor for the series. Rabbis Steven M. Reuben, Howard O. Laibson, Emily Feigenson, Ronald Mass, Nina Mizrahi, Paul Yedwab, Jeffrey Perry-Marx, Gary Bretton-Granatoor, and Herman Snyder made particularly significant comments over the years, as did Edith Samuel ז״ל and Judith Spiegler Paskind.

Finally, no individual contributed more to this book than my secretary, Eppie Begleiter. She typed each article with painstaking attention, always encouraging, always caring. She is a special treasure.

Photo credits

Abramson, H.R., p. 106
Bell, Cynthia, designer, p.85
Boston Globe/Frank O'Brien, p. 72
Design Photographers International/Jack Mitchell, p. 15
Eichenbaum, Rose, p. 12
Israel Government Press Office, pp. 36, 42, 44
Israel Information Service, p. 51
Israel Office of Information, p. 55
Jewish Museum, N.Y., pp. 81, 87
Jewish Theological Seminary of America, N.Y./Frank J.
 Darmstaedter, pp. 4, 8, 25, 31
Knight, Leo, p. 74
Moon, Anna Kaufman, p. 91
Moriah Antique Judaica, p. 59
Mula and Haramaty, p. 82
N.Y. Public Library Picture Collection, p. 64
Schlesinger, F., p. 122
The Second Jewish Catalog, reprint, p. 96
Weiss, K., p. 52
Zwerin, Edward, p. 3

Contents

Introduction

The observance of ceremonies is an essential element of religious life. There can be no creed without its forms. The pure idea can serve only a few rare individuals—theologians, philosophers, if you will. The truth—to be felt by most of us—must put on a garb. There must be rite, legend, ceremony, visible form.

Even so it is with Judaism. To be a Jew in one's mind and heart is simply not sufficient for the need. The rites of our faith embody its ideas and ideals, as well as our people's history. And only by observing them can we secure our creative continuity.

Form can stifle substance, to be sure. Rituals performed by rote are ineffectual. They become spiritless, devoid of life. But they are "empty" only to those who see them but with their eyes, who fail to understand the ideas, the values, the hopes they express and who do not know the circumstances that brought them to be.

This is precisely why Dan Syme's *The Jewish Home* is of such worth. It describes not only how the holiday and life cycle rites of Judaism are to be observed, but also the concepts they symbolize and the historic events that brought them to be.

Based on his informative columns first published in *Reform Judaism*, the volume before us can serve as an introduction to Judaism for Jews-by-choice and birth alike. The felicitous question-and-answer approach makes this work eminently readable and useful, both in the class setting and for individual study.

Properly, the author focuses on home observances. Their celebration will enhance the Jewishness of our families in their dwellings and, in this manner, assure our continuity. After all, the Jewish home, no less than the synagogue, is a magic ingredient of our people's wondrous endurance.

Alexander M. Schindler

·1·

THE MEZUZAH

1. What is a mezuzah?

The Hebrew word *mezuzah* means "doorpost." According to tradition, the *mezuzah* is to be affixed to the doorpost at the entrance to a Jewish home as well as at the entrance to each of the interior rooms except for bathrooms.

The *mezuzah* itself consists of a small scroll of parchment (*klaf*) on which are written two biblical passages, Deuteronomy 6:4–9 and Deuteronomy 11:13–21. This scroll is then inserted into a wooden, plastic, or metal casing which is often quite beautiful and artistic in design. A *mezuzah* may be purchased at any store which handles Jewish religious articles.

2. Why do Jews affix a mezuzah to the doorpost of a home?

The custom of affixing a *mezuzah* to the doorpost fulfills the biblical commandment: "You shall write them upon the doorposts of thy house and upon thy gates" (Deuteronomy 6:9). The *mezuzah* distinguishes a Jewish home and is a visible sign and symbol to all those who enter that a sense of Jewish identity and commitment exists in that household.

3. Can we make our own mezuzah?

Tradition requires a certain form for the scroll (*klaf*) but not for the casing. The casing, then, may certainly be designed and created by the family. The scroll, however, should be purchased and placed inside.

4. How do we go about affixing the mezuzah to the doorpost?

This should be a family ceremony, with all family members present. The ceremony begins with a blessing: *Baruch Atah Adonai Elohenu Melech ha'olam asher kidshanu bemitzvotav vetzivanu likboa mezuzah.* "Blessed are You, O Lord our God, King of the universe, who has sanctified us by commandments and commanded us to affix a *mezuzah.*"

After the blessing is recited, the *mezuzah* is attached to the doorpost with nails, glue, or screws, on the right side of the door as one enters the room.

Position the *mezuzah* about a third of the way down from the top of the doorpost. Sephardic Jews usually angle the *mezuzah* with the top tilted inwards towards the interior of the house or room, while Ashkenazim commonly place the *mezuzah* in an upright position.

·2·
SHABBAT

Shabbat Candles

1. Why do we light Shabbat candles?

The lighting of candles ushers in Shabbat. The practice is a rabbinic institution which, over the centuries, has acquired the force of law.

2. Who may light Shabbat candles?

Jewish tradition requires the woman of the household to light the Shabbat candles, beginning on the first Shabbat after her marriage. However, should no woman be present, a man must light the Shabbat candles himself, since the lighting of candles is a requirement of Shabbat observance, not necessarily tied to gender.

3. How many candles do we light?

Jewish law requires a minimum of two candles, since the fourth of the Ten Commandments occurs in two separate sections of the Torah in different form:

    a. Remember the Sabbath day to keep it holy.

    b. Observe the Sabbath day to keep it holy.

More than two candles may be kindled, but the usual number is two.

4. Are there any restrictions as to color or shape of the candles to be used for Shabbat?

No. It is customary to use white candles made especially for Shabbat, but candles of any color may be utilized so long as they will burn for a substantial length of time into the evening.

5. When do we light the Shabbat candles?

Orthodox Jews light Shabbat candles approximately 15–20 minutes before sundown. During the summer, Shabbat candles are often lit somewhat earlier, since nightfall comes so late in the evening. Jewish tradition dictates, however, that no candles are to be lit once sundown passes.

This Orthodox practice is not strictly observed in Reform Jewish homes, where Shabbat candles are usually lit immediately prior to the Shabbat meal, whether before or after sunset.

6. How do we light the Shabbat candles?

The laws of Shabbat prohibit the lighting of any fire once Shabbat begins. Thus, we light the candles *before* saying the blessing, since the blessing marks the beginning of Shabbat.

However, since a blessing always *precedes* an act, we cover our eyes while reciting the blessing so as not to view the burning candles until after the blessing has been completed.

The procedure, then, is as follows:

    a. Light the candles.

    b. Cover or close the eyes.

    c. Recite the blessing: *Baruch Atah Adonai Elohenu Melech ha'olam asher kidshanu bemitzvotav vetzivanu lehadlik ner shel Shabbat.*

"Blessed are You, O Lord our God, King of the universe, who has sanctified us by commandments and commanded us to kindle the Shabbat candle."

The Friday Night Shabbat Kiddush

1. What does the word kiddush mean?

Kiddush means "sanctification." It comes from the same Hebrew root as the word *kadosh,* which means "holy."

2. Why do we recite the kiddush on Shabbat?

The Book of Exodus 20:8 contains the fourth of the commandments: "Remember the Sabbath day to keep it holy" (to sanctify it). The rabbis interpreted the word "remember" as an injunction to sanctify Shabbat both at its beginning and its end. The *Havdalah* service fulfills the mitzvah at the conclusion of Shabbat, the *kiddush* at its beginning.

3. Why do we recite the kiddush over wine?

Wine is a symbol of joy and life in Judaism. While no specific reference to wine in relation to *kiddush* appears in the Torah, the rabbis declared that the *kiddush* should be recited over wine (". . . *Boray peri hagafen*"). Out of sensitivity to those who had no wine, however, the rabbis also ruled that the *kiddush* may be recited over the *chalah.* In such a case, the *Motzi* is substituted for the prayer over the wine.

4. Who recites the kiddush?

While it is customary for at least one adult male to recite the *kiddush,* this ritual is a requirement of Shabbat itself and not necessarily the sole domain of men or women. In the absence of an adult male, a woman recites or chants the *kiddush.* In addition, all those who are present at the table should join in the *kiddush,* if they so desire.

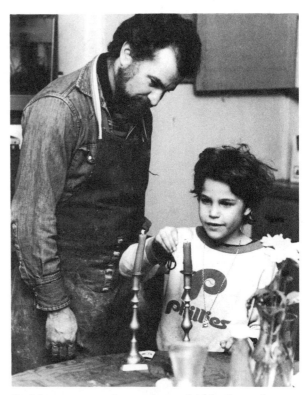

5. May any cup be used as a kiddush cup?

There is no prescribed form or design for the *kiddush* cup. Custom has resulted in beautiful cups being designed especially for Shabbat, so as to honor the Shabbat and its special significance. But any cup or glass may be used, the only traditional requirement being that it contain at least 3.3 ounces of wine.

6. Can we use any kind of wine for kiddush?

No. Not if you adhere to tradition. The *berachah* ". . . *Boray peri hagafen*" refers to the fruit of the vine. This means that the wine must be made from grapes and not other fruits. Then, too, the wine should be kosher. If there are members of the family who are not allowed to drink wine for reasons of health, they may recite the *kiddush* over grape juice. This, too, should be kosher if strict traditional practice is followed. Reform Jewish families may or may not observe *kashrut* and therefore use kosher or non-kosher wine and grape juice as they choose.

7. What is the structure of the Shabbat kiddush?

The traditional Shabbat *kiddush* consists of three sections:

a. A section from the creation story in the Torah describing how God rested on the seventh day, blessed it, and hallowed it (Genesis 1:31–2:3).

b. A blessing over the wine.

c. A blessing over Shabbat itself.

8. Why does the blessing over the wine precede the blessing over Shabbat?

There is a beautiful story which some say explains this order. The rich people and the poor people had an argument over which *berachah* should come first. The rich people said: "The blessing over Shabbat should come first. What is wine? We can have wine every day of the week if we wish!" The poor people said: "The blessing over the wine should come first. Shabbat is special to us. We wish to honor it. But, for us, wine is a sacrifice. We have to save and scrimp to have our wine for Shabbat. Have respect for our sacrifice. Put the blessing over the wine first." The rabbis debated. Finally, it was decided that the blessing over the wine should come first, out of respect to the sacrifice of the poor.

For a full text of the *kiddush* as recited in Reform households (Hebrew, English, and transliteration), see pp. 776–7 of *Gates of Prayer*, published by the Central Conference of American Rabbis.

The Shabbat Chalah

1. What does the Hebrew word chalah mean?

Chalah means "dough" and refers to the special twisted loaf of bread eaten by Jews on Shabbat and other special occasions.

2. Why do we say a blessing over the chalah?

Jewish tradition calls for a *berachah* expressing thanks to God before eating any food. It represents a recognition that people owe a measure of gratitude to God for providing food for all living things.

In addition, some feel that we say a *berachah* before eating in order to indicate the distinction between human beings and animals. Set a plate of food before a hungry beast and the animal will tear into it without hesitation. People say a blessing, both before and after eating.

3. It is traditional to use two chalot on Shabbat. Why?

Tradition holds that two whole *chalot* should be used on Shabbat as a remembrance of the double portion of manna which fell in the desert so that no Jew should have to gather food on Shabbat (Exodus 16:22–32). Another interpretation is that the two *chalot* fulfill the biblical injunction articulated in the two versions of the Ten Commandments in the Torah: "*Remember* the Sabbath day to keep it holy" (Exodus 20:8) and "*Observe* the Sabbath day to keep it holy" (Deuteronomy 5:12).

4. The chalot and the knife with which we slice them are covered before the blessing. Why?

The rabbis used the *chalah* as a vehicle to teach two important Jewish values: human dignity and the preciousness of peace.

is covered, then, to remove from sight any visible token of violence in the world. There is another tradition that no knife at all should be used, as a reminder of the prophetic verse: "And they shall beat their swords into plowshares and their spears into pruning hooks" (Isaiah 2:4). The *chalot* are then broken apart by hand, with pieces distributed to all present. Whatever the practice, however, the lesson of the preciousness of peace is paramount.

5. **How do we bless the chalot?**
    a. Usually the head of the household uncovers the *chalot* and recites the *Motzi* blessing as follows: *Baruch Atah Adonai Elohenu Melech ha'olam hamotzi lechem min ha'aretz.* "Blessed are You, O Lord our God, Ruler of the world, who brings forth bread out of the earth." Others sitting at the table should either join in reciting the blessing or answer "amen" at its conclusion.
    b. The *chalot* are then sliced or broken apart, with pieces distributed to all present.
    c. Before eating the *chalah*, it is also traditional to salt it. There are two explanations for this practice. One interpretation is that salt is a spice and thus appropriate to use on the special eve of Shabbat. Others explained that the salt reminded family members of the biblical verse "by the sweat of your brow shall you get bread to eat" (Genesis 3:19).

As one looks at the Shabbat table, one notices that the Shabbat candles are in beautiful candlesticks and that the wine is held up in a lovely *kiddush* cup. While the *berachot* over them are being recited, the *chalah* lies alone on the table. The rabbis, seeing this, decreed that the *chalah* should be covered, lest its feelings be hurt by its seemingly secondary status. One rabbi said: "This teaches us concern for the feelings even of inanimate things. And if this is the case, how much more so we should be concerned about the feelings of human beings." Thus, we cover the *chalot* as a lesson in human dignity.

But why cover the knife? The knife is seen as a weapon of war and violence. On Shabbat, our thoughts are of peace and harmony. The knife

The *chalah* thus serves as a tangible symbol of the Jewish values of gratitude to God, the uniqueness of people, the quest for peace, and the dignity and worth of every individual—all important and appropriate themes for Shabbat.

Blessing One's Children on Shabbat

There is a Jewish custom in which parents bless their children on Shabbat. This beautiful tradition derives from one of the most touching of biblical stories.

We all know how Joseph was sold into slavery by his brothers (Genesis 37). The brothers lied to Jacob, his father, and told Jacob that Joseph had been killed by a wild beast. Years later, Joseph, who was by now governor over Egypt, was reunited with his brothers in a beautiful biblical tale of sibling reconciliation (Genesis 45). Joseph then brought his father to Egypt in order to care for him in his last years.

When Jacob lay on his death bed, he summoned

Joseph in order to bless him. Joseph entered with his two sons, Ephraim and Menasseh, whom Jacob had never seen. The Torah records this touching scene in Genesis 48:8–11, 20:

"And Israel (another name for Jacob) beheld Joseph's sons and said: 'Who are these?' And Joseph said unto his father: 'They are my sons, whom God hath given me here.' And he said: 'Bring them, I pray thee, unto me, and I will bless them.'

"Now the eyes of Israel were dim for age, so that he could not see. And he brought them near unto him and kissed them and embraced them. And Israel said unto Joseph: 'I thought that I would never see your face again; but God has let me see your children also.'

"And he blessed them that day, saying: 'By you shall Israel (the Jewish people) bless, saying: God make you as Ephraim and as Menasseh'.'"

We relive the story of the blessing of the children through a simple Shabbat ceremony, just after blessing the candles and before the *kiddush*. The parent places both hands on the child's bowed head and recites the following blessing:

(For sons)
Yesimcha Elohim ke'efrayim vechimenasheh. "May God make you as Ephraim and Menasseh."

(For daughters)
Yesimech Elohim kesarah, Rivkah, Rachel, veleah. "May God make you as Sarah, Rebecca, Rachel, and Leah." (These are the four matriarchs of Jewish history.)

The parent then pronounces the traditional threefold benediction over all the children together: *Yevarechecha Adonai veyishmerecha. Yaer Adonai panav elecha vichuneka. Yisa Adonai panav elecha veyasem lecha shalom.* "May the Lord bless you and care for you." "May the Lord cause the light of His countenance to shine upon you and be gracious unto you." "May the Lord lift up His countenance upon you and give you peace."

If there are memories which last a lifetime, a parent's blessing is surely one of them. Perhaps this ritual, so often neglected—and even forgotten—should become part of your family's Shabbat celebration.

Shabbat Havdalah

1. What is the meaning of Havdalah?

Havdalah is a Hebrew word meaning "division" or "separation" and is also the name of a special and beautiful ritual which, according to tradition, formally ends the Shabbat, "separating" it from the beginning of the new week. The *Havdalah* ritual is now observed in a growing number of Reform Jewish homes. Its popularity in Reform Judaism has emerged primarily through its extensive practice in North American Federation of Temple Youth conclaves, retreats, and camp activities.

2. When does the Havdalah ritual take place?

According to Orthodox practice, the *Havdalah* prayers are recited both in the synagogue, after the Saturday *Ma'ariv* (evening) service, and in the home, so that all members of the family may participate. The traditional *Havdalah* begins any time after nightfall and, according to Orthodox tradition, may be recited until the following Tuesday evening. Where *Havdalah* is observed in Reform Jewish homes, it is almost always on Saturday evening.

3. Who recites the Havdalah prayers?

It is customary for an adult male to recite *Havdalah*. But, like so many other rituals, *Havdalah* is a traditional requirement of Shabbat itself and thus not tied to one sex. Both men and women may recite *Havdalah*.

4. What is the origin of Havdalah?

Havdalah, according to tradition, was instituted by the "Men of the Great Synagogue." Its basis in *halachah* derives from the fourth of the Ten Commandments: "Remember the Sabbath day to sanctify it" (Exodus 20:8). The rabbis decided that "remembering" Shabbat required "sanctifying it" both at its beginning (*kiddush*) and its end (*Havdalah*).

5. What is the structure of the Havdalah ritual?

The traditional *Havdalah* ritual has five parts:

a. An introductory Hebrew paragraph praising God, with a theme of salvation, including verses from Isaiah, Psalms, and the Book of Esther.

b. A blessing over a cup of wine: *Baruch Atah Adonai Elohenu Melech ha'olam bore peri hagafen.* "Blessed are You, O Lord our God, Ruler of the universe, Creator of the fruit of the vine."

c. A blessing over fragrant spices (*besamim*) in a special spice box: *Baruch Atah Adonai Elohenu Melech ha'olam bore mine besamim.* "Blessed are You, O Lord our God, Ruler of the universe, Creator of many kinds of spices."

d. A blessing over light, using a special braided *Havdalah* candle with two or more wicks: *Baruch Atah Adonai Elohenu Melech ha'olam bore me'ore ha'esh.* "Blessed are You, O Lord our God, Ruler of the universe, Creator of the lights of the fire."

e. A final prayer whose major theme is the distinction between the holiness of Shabbat and the rest of the days of the week: *Baruch Atah Adonai Elohenu Melech ha'olam hamavdil beyn kodesh lechol beyn or lechoshech beyn Yisrael leamim beyn yom hashevi'i lesheshet yeme hama'aseh. Baruch Atah Adonai hamavdil beyn kodesh lechol.* "Blessed are You, O Lord our God, Ruler of the universe, who makes a distinction between the holy and the secular, between light and darkness, between Israel and the other nations, between the seventh day and the six working days. Blessed are You, O Lord our God, who makes a distinction between the holy and the secular."

In many homes, three melodies are chanted at the conclusion of the ritual:

a. A melody based on the *Hamavdil* prayer.
b. *Eliahu Ha-navi* (Elijah the Prophet)
c. *Shavua Tov* (A Good Week)

6. Why a paragraph on salvation in a ritual ending Shabbat?

First of all, it is rather common for verses from Scripture to precede ritual in Judaism. For example, we saw how a paragraph from the Genesis creation story precedes the Shabbat *kiddush.*

Secondly, traditional Jews saw God as the Protector from whatever problems or crises might ensue in the coming week. Thus, a new week began with thanks to God for past blessings and an expression of trust in God for future days.

7. Why a blessing over wine?

While the blessing over wine fulfills the biblical injunction to "remember" the Shabbat, the use of wine was instituted by the rabbis, chosen as a symbol of life and joy.

Out of respect to the poor or to those who might have no wine, however, tradition allows any other beverage—other than water—to be used. The appropriate blessing over that particular beverage is then recited.

8. Why a blessing over spices?

According to rabbinic legend, each Jew receives an additional soul on Shabbat (*neshamah yeterah*). At the end of Shabbat, the extra soul departs.

The smelling of fragrant spices (*besamim*) thus became a symbolic way of refreshing the remaining soul and compensating the individual Jew for the loss of extra spiritual strength.

The spices are usually contained in a special *besamim* box made of silver, wood, or some other material. Beautiful *besamim* boxes have been created by Jews for centuries. You can make your own if you so desire.

9. Why a blessing over light and especially over a braided candle?

Light was God's first creation, according to the Torah. Therefore, tradition deemed it appropriate to begin a new week by blessing light. Also, light is a symbol of God's presence and of the divine potential in every human being.

The special braided candle arose out of a rabbinic interpretation of the blessing over the light. Since the literal translation is "Creator of the lights [plural] of fire," the rabbis ruled that there must be at least two candles with two wicks. Hence the braided *Havdalah* candle. Where one is not available, two ordinary candles may be used, so long as the flames from the two wicks are joined in a single flame.

10. What is the order of the traditional home Havdalah service?

a. A member of the family (usually a child) is given the *Havdalah* candle to hold.

b. The leader of the service fills the wine cup to the brim, lights the *Havdalah* candle, and recites the blessing over the wine. He or she does not drink the wine at this time.

c. The leader picks up the *besamim* box and recites the blessing over the fragrant spices. He or she then smells them and passes the *besamim* box to other members of the family so that they can smell them as well.

d. The blessing over the *Havdalah* candle is recited. While doing so, the leader customarily looks at his or her hands or fingernails in the light of the flame.

e. The *Hamavdil* prayer is recited.

f. The leader pours a few drops of wine onto a dish and extinguishes the candle in the wine.

g. The leader drinks from the cup of wine and passes it around to other family members

as they sing: (1) *Hamavdil,* (2) *Eliahu Ha-navi,* and (3) *Shavua Tov.*

11. Why do we look at our hands in the light of the candle?

It is traditional not to recite a blessing "in vain," without using some of that which we bless. Hence the custom of "using" the light of the candle.

12. Why do we sing "Eliahu Ha-navi" and "Shavua Tov"?

For Orthodox Jews, Elijah's coming will herald the coming of the Messiah. For Reform Jews, Elijah symbolizes the hope for a messianic age, when all people will work together for a better world. Thus, as a suitable conclusion to Shabbat, *Shavua Tov* (a good week) is combined with expression of hope for a just and peaceful society.

For the full text of *Havdalah* as recited in Reform households (Hebrew, English, and transliteration), see *Gates of Prayer,* published by the Central Conference of American Rabbis.

·3·

PESACH

Some Background

The observance of any holiday is made more meaningful by an understanding of its origins. This is especially true of Pesach, perhaps the most beloved of all Jewish festivals and certainly possessing the most elaborate home ritual of any Jewish holiday. As we shall see, the themes of freedom, Jewish continuity, and the potential for a just and peaceful world are plentifully illustrated through song and symbol, prayer and historical memory.

1. What is Pesach?

Pesach is a major Jewish spring festival, commemorating the Exodus from Egypt over 3,000 years ago, whose ritual observance centers around a special home service (the seder), the prohibition of leaven (*chametz*), and the eating of matzah.

2. How did Pesach, or Passover, get its name?

Actually, Pesach has five different names, each of which carries a special significance:
   a. Chag Ha-Matzot (The Festival of Unleavened Bread).
   b. Chag Ha-Pesach (The Festival of Paschal Offering).
   c. Chag Ha-Aviv (The Festival of Spring).
   d. Zeman Cherutenu (The Season of Our Liberation).
   e. Pesach (Passover).

3. Why is Pesach called Chag Ha-Matzot?

The name Chag Ha-Matzot has both agricultural and historical origins. Scholars of ancient civilizations tell us that, prior to the Exodus from Egypt, certain peoples would harvest their spring barley crops and bake the first fruits thereof into special unleavened cakes. These cakes were then eaten as part of a ceremony expressing gratitude to their deity for an abundant crop.

As a primarily agricultural society, ancient Israel shared this custom, investing it with powerful historical significance. You will recall that the Jews had to leave Egypt in great haste. Exodus 12:34 records that, as a result, "the people took their dough before it was leavened." Later, in Exodus 12:39, the text relates that "they baked unleavened cakes of the dough which they brought forth out of Egypt, for it was not leavened; because they were thrust out of Egypt, and could not tarry." Finally, in Exodus 23:15, the historical bond is forged: "The feast of unleavened bread (Chag Ha-Matzot) shalt thou keep; seven days thou shalt eat unleavened bread, as I commanded thee . . . for . . . thou camest out from Egypt."

4. Why is Pesach called Chag Ha-Pesach?

The name Chag Ha-Pesach also has agricultural and historical associations. According to some scholars, an ancient practice of primitive peoples involved sacrificing one lamb from each flock in order to please their deity and thereby, presum-

Searching for leaven. Engraving by Bernard Picart, 1725.

ably, to protect the rest of the flock from harm. This paschal offering or "pesach" became a pivotal element in the Exodus account.

During the night of the tenth plague, which witnessed the death of every Egyptian first-born son, the blood of a sacrificed lamb, smeared on the doorpost of every Jewish home, safeguarded the homes from the angel of death. Exodus 12:11 states: "It is the Pesach of the Lord." Verse 14 continues: "And this day shall be to you one of remembrance; you shall celebrate it as a festival to the Lord throughout the ages; you shall celebrate it as an institution for all time." And Exodus 34:25 specifically alludes to the Festival of Pesach (Chag Pesach). Thus, a second name for Passover evolved from a primitive agricultural rite into a historical symbol.

5. Why is Pesach called Chag Ha-Aviv?

Pesach is called the Festival of Spring because it always falls in April or May of the secular calendar year. The Hebrew calendar date for the beginning of Pesach is the fifteenth of Nisan. Differences in the lunar (Jewish) and solar (secular)

calendars account for time variations from year to year.

Exodus 12:6 and 12:18 pinpoint the fifteenth day of Nisan as the holiday's date. And Exodus 13:4 designates the "month of Aviv" (Nisan) as the designated lunar month. Hence, Chag Ha-Aviv became a third name for Passover.

6. Why is Pesach called Zeman Cherutenu?

It was the particular genius of Judaism to be able to take elements from three essentially agricultural festivals and mold them into a holiday celebrating the freedom of a people. The Exodus, the Festival of Matzot, the paschal offering, and the festive seder meal came to be a paradigm for liberation from tyranny and oppression.

Pesach endured through the time of Joshua (Joshua 5:10–11). Hundreds of years later, King Josiah was still instructing the people as to its observance (II Kings 23:21–23). The holiday and its powerful message continued to stir the Jewish soul. And so it was only natural that, in the first few centuries C.E., an evolving rabbinic literature captured its essence by referring to it as Zeman

Cherutenu, the Season of Our Liberation. As Moses said to the people: "Remember this day, on which you went free from Egypt, the house of bondage" (Exodus 13:3).

7. Why did Pesach, or Passover, emerge as the most popular name for the holiday?

This final name derives from Exodus 12:23, an account of how Moses promised the Israelites that God would "pass over" their homes during the terrible night of the slaying of the Egyptian first-born. Pesach, or Passover, ultimately became the name which unified the many concepts embodied by the holiday. It endured throughout the rabbinic period and to this day.

8. For how many days do we celebrate Pesach?

The Torah commands an observance of seven days (Exodus 12:15; 13:6). Reform Jews and all Jews in Israel follow this injunction. Conservative and Orthodox Jews outside the land of Israel, however, celebrate Pesach for eight days. The additional day of observance dates back to 700–600 B.C.E. At that time, people were notified of a holiday's beginning by means of an elaborate network of mountaintop bonfires. To guard against the possibility of error, an extra day was added to many of the holidays. By the time a dependable calendar came into existence, around the fourth century C.E., the additional day was so deeply engrained in the observance of Diaspora Jewry that the talmudic sages made the practice *halachah,* law.

Whether seven or eight days, Pesach has many beautiful rituals, symbols, songs, and stories, which every Jew may learn and enjoy.

Chametz

1. What is chametz?

Chametz is a Hebrew word meaning "leaven." It is also the generic term for a class of foods which are traditionally prohibited during the holiday of Pesach. Rabbinic authorities defined *chametz* as any leavened product of five grains: wheat, oats, barley, rye, and spelt. Ashkenazic Jews later added rice, corn, peas, beans, and peanuts to those foods classified as *chametz.*

2. Why is chametz prohibited during Pesach?

The Torah specifically mentions *chametz* in three passages in the Book of Exodus. Excommunication was the severe punishment for consuming, carrying, or even owning *chametz* during Pesach. The disproportionate emphasis given to *chametz* in the Torah has led some scholars to theorize that this prohibition was originally a primitive, powerful ritual taboo. Later rabbinic authorities softened the penalties relating to *chametz,* but there is no doubt that the laws were strictly observed and taken seriously.

As a result, three interesting customs evolved among traditional Jews, all directly tied to the *chametz* prohibitions:

a. *Bedikat chametz:* the search for leaven.
b. *Biur chametz:* the burning of leaven.
c. *Mechirat chametz:* the sale of leaven.

3. What is bedikat chametz?

Jews who strictly observe Pesach undertake a thorough cleaning of their homes just prior to the holiday, removing or setting aside all leaven in the process.

On the night before the first seder, the Mishnah ordains a formal search for leaven in the home. A blessing is recited, then the head of the household, usually accompanied by the rest of the family, moves from room to room. The house is darkened. The individual conducting the search carries a candle, a wooden spoon, and a feather. As preplaced pieces of bread (usually ten) are discovered, they are swept into the spoon with the feather. When the search is completed, a special statement of nullification is recited, indicating that the house is now free of *chametz.*

While this ceremony is not observed in most Reform Jewish homes, it reflects a serious commitment to the traditional laws of Pesach and is an impressive experience for young children. You may wish to consider it for personal observance.

4. What is biur chametz?

On the morning after the *bedikat chametz*, tradition calls for a simple ceremony wherein the *chametz*, gathered the previous evening, is burned. The statement of nullification is repeated. In traditional homes, this ceremony takes place before 10:00 a.m., after which no *chametz* is eaten until the end of Pesach. Most Reform Jews do not observe this ritual.

5. What is mechirat chametz?

While the law calls for the physical removal of all personally-owned leaven from the home, the rabbis realized that this practice would impose a financial hardship upon those families who had substantial amounts of *chametz* products in their households. Therefore, the custom evolved of simply placing all leaven in a secluded part of the home and selling it, on paper, to a non-Jew. As the law did not prohibit the presence of *chametz* in the home of non-Jews, this practice did not compromise the law. At the conclusion of the holiday, the leaven was then repurchased by the family. At first, each family handled its own sale. Eventually, however, it became common for a single Jew, usually the rabbi, to conduct a single transaction on behalf of the entire community. In most Reform homes, leavened products are simply set aside for the duration of Pesach, without the formal act of *mechirat chametz*.

Thus, we see that the prohibition against leaven was concretized in a number of elaborate ritual and ceremonial acts. Just as important, however, was the commandment to eat unleavened bread, matzah.

Matzah

1. What is matzah?

Matzah is the Hebrew word for "unleavened bread" and refers to the special waferlike food eaten by Jews, particularly on Pesach.

2. What is the origin of matzah?

The earliest mention of matzah in the Torah occurs in Exodus 12:15. I Samuel 28:24 also relates a story in which matzah was served to King Saul by the woman at En-Dor. In this later instance, it is clear that matzah was a food hastily prepared for unexpected guests, allowing no time for leavening. Hence the term matzah, or unleavened bread.

3. How did matzah come to be associated with Pesach?

Three passages in the Book of Exodus specifically command the eating of matzah during Pesach. The penalty for transgressing this *mitzvah*, cited in the Torah, is excommunication, especially if *chametz* was consumed instead of matzah. Modern Jews reject this severe approach.

The historical tie between Pesach and matzah is articulated in Exodus 12:34–39 and Deuteronomy 16:3. In the former instance, it is implied that we eat matzah as a reminder of the haste

with which our ancestors had to leave Egypt, leaving them no time to bake leavened bread. The Deuteronomy passage and the *haggadah* refer to matzah as the "bread of affliction," alluding to the simple fare of the Jewish slaves in Egypt, and establishing matzah as a symbol of oppression. In short, then, the practice of eating matzah during Pesach is Torah-based, as are its symbolic and historical bonds.

4. How is matzah made?

Matzah is the unleavened product of one of five grains: wheat, oats, barley, spelt, or rye. Wheat, though, is most commonly used in making matzah. Until the nineteenth century, matzah was prepared exclusively by hand and baked in special ovens. The first matzah-baking machine was invented in 1857 in Austria. Since that time, matzah has been made by hand or machine, depending on its type.

5. What are the various types of matzah?

There are three basic types of matzah:

a. Matzah shemurah ("watched" or "guarded" matzah).

Shemurah matzah is so called because the grain used to prepare it is watched from the time it is harvested until it is actually baked. This "watching" assures that the grain does not come into contact with any moisture or heat and thus initiate the leavening process. It is usually prepared by hand and the entire process, from kneading the dough to finished product, must not exceed eighteen minutes. A longer time span is considered to render the dough leavened, thus making it unsuitable for Pesach. This type of matzah is eaten mostly by traditional Jews, especially during the two seders. Other types of matzah are then eaten during the rest of the holiday.

b. Regular matzah.

The most common type of matzah is not as stringently supervised as shemurah matzah, being watched only from the time of milling, rather than from the harvest. Regular matzah is usually made by machine, rather than by hand, although the eighteen-minute time limit is also observed by companies using a machine-baking process. Traditional Jews usually eat regular matzah throughout Pesach, except for the two seders, while most Reform Jewish families eat regular matzah during the entire holiday.

c. Enriched matzah.

Many matzah companies enrich matzah by adding eggs, fruit, juice, milk, and wine, so that Jews who need more nutrition than that afforded by regular matzah might not have to violate the prohibition against *chametz* for reasons of health. Enriched matzah, however, does not fulfill the commandment of eating matzah on Pesach. Consequently, those Jews who do eat it usually partake of shemurah or regular matzah at the seder.

6. Does matzah have a required shape?

No. Until the advent of the matzah-baking machine, most matzah was round. This practice derived from Exodus 12:39, which required the eating of *uggot* matzah. In Hebrew, the word *uggot* means "cakes," but it has an additional meaning of "circles." Thus, most Jews baked matzah according to this linguistic interpretation. Modern technology dictated a square shape for matzah, since the early machines could not be tooled for circular cakes. There is, however, no prescribed shape for matzah, and most Jews today consume either the round or square variety.

7. When do we eat matzah?

Jewish law dictates that one should refrain from eating matzah for at least a day preceding the seder so as to heighten one's enjoyment at the meal. The law only requires matzah consumption at the seder itself. At all other times during the holiday, the eating of matzah is optional. *Chametz*, however, is not to be consumed at any time during Pesach.

The seder service includes the eating of matzah at many different moments.

The Seder Table

As the time for the seder approaches, after the house has been cleaned and the *chametz* removed, be sure that your seder table includes the following:

1. A haggadah for each participant.

The Central Conference of American Rabbis has published a *haggadah* for use in Reform households. Beautifully illustrated by Leonard Baskin, the *CCAR Haggadah* is a must for every Reform Jewish home. Copies may be secured through your congregation or by writing to the CCAR at 192 Lexington Avenue, Rooms 701–2, NYC 10016.

2. Festival candles and candlesticks.

3. A kiddush cup and wine for the festival kiddush.

In addition, every participant should have his or her own wine glass. We drink four cups of wine during the seder service as a remembrance of the four promises which the Torah tells us God made to our people in Egypt: "I will bring you out"; "I will deliver you"; "I will redeem you"; "I will take you to me for a people" (Exodus 6:6–7). Many Reform Jews add a fifth cup of wine, calling to mind the plight of Soviet Jewry and/ or our commitment to the State of Israel.

4. Elijah's cup.

We will examine special seder rituals, such as opening the door for Elijah, shortly. For now, suffice it to say that liberal Jews consider Elijah to be a symbol of a potential Messianic Age. We thus set aside a special cup as an expression of our hope and confidence in the ultimate betterment of society.

5. Three whole matzot.

Three whole matzot should be set before the leader of the seder. Jewish custom has been that these matzot are contained in a special three-section matzah cover.

Why three? The top and bottom matzot correspond to the two *chalot* which tradition ordains for Shabbat, an extra portion for a special day.

The third piece represents the matzah which Jewish law specifically ordains for Pesach.

Half of this third or middle matzah also serves as the *afikoman,* or dessert, which is hidden away as the object of a search by children at the seder. Over the centuries, the three matzot have acquired special symbolic associations. Some say they represent the three patriarchs, Abraham, Isaac, and Jacob. Others associate the matzot with the three categories of Jews in ancient times, *kohen,* Levite, and Israelite.

6. The seder plate.

The seder plate, also placed before the leader, contains the various symbolic foods referred to in the seder itself.

a. A roasted shankbone.
   Symbolic of the paschal offering brought to the Temple in Jerusalem in ancient times. Many Jews also see the shankbone as a symbol of God's "outstretched arm," helping the Jewish people in times of trouble. It is of interest to note that the Samaritans and Falashas in the Middle East and Africa, even today, sacrifice a lamb on Pesach.

b. Maror or bitter herbs.
   Usually a horseradish root or romaine lettuce, symbolic of the bitterness our ancestors experienced as slaves in Egypt.

c. Karpas.
   A vegetable, usually parsley, symbolic of spring and its spirit of hope, as well as the Jew's undying faith in the future. Any green vegetable is permitted, and many Jews use lettuce or celery instead of parsley.

d. A roasted egg.

Traditionally a symbol of the continuing cycle of life. It also reminds us of the special festival offering brought to the Temple in Jerusalem in ancient times. In addition, some see the egg as a symbol of the Jewish people's will to survive. Just as an egg becomes harder the longer it cooks, so the Jewish people have emerged from the crucible of persecution as a strong and living people.

e. Charoset.
Usually a combination of apples, wine, walnuts, and cinnamon which symbolizes the mortar that our ancestors used to make bricks in Egypt.

f. A dish of salt water.
Symbolic of the tears our ancestors shed in Egypt.

Tradition does not dictate the shape or size of the seder plate. Many families purchase one of the beautifully artistic seder plates made in Israel, but it may be round or square, plain or ornate.

7. Symbolic foods for each participant.
Because the seder actively involves every member of the family, certain foods should be at each place setting.

a. A wine cup
b. Matzah
c. Maror (usually horseradish)
d. Charoset
e. Salt water
f. Karpas (usually parsley)
g. A hard-boiled egg

The Seder

1. What does seder mean?
The Hebrew word seder means "order" and refers to the religious service and festive meal observed in Jewish households on Pesach. Seder derives from the same root as the Hebrew word *siddur* (prayer book). Just as the *siddur* contains the order of prayers for daily, Shabbat, and festival services, so is the seder a prescribed order of prayers, readings, symbolic explanations, and songs related to Pesach. The Pesach seder is the only ritual meal in the Jewish calendar year for which such an order is prescribed. Hence its name.

2. Does the seder have biblical origins?
Yes. The seder has a number of scriptural bases. Exodus 12:3–11 describes the meal of lamb, unleavened bread, and bitter herbs which the Israelites ate just prior to the Exodus. In addition, three separate passages in Exodus (12:26–27, 13:8, 13:14) and one in Deuteronomy (6:20–21) enunciate the duty of parents to tell the story of the Exodus to their children. We also know that a special meal was connected with the paschal offer-

ing which Jews of ancient times brought to the Temple in Jerusalem on Pesach.

The meal, the symbols, and the retelling of the Exodus account eventually became basic elements of the seder as we know it today.

3. When did the seder as celebrated in modern times begin to take shape?

Around the year 70 C.E., when the Temple in Jerusalem was destroyed by the Romans. With the priestly paschal sacrifice and meal no longer possible, and with the Jewish community in exile and in ritual upheaval, a new religious service, the seder, emerged as a means of preserving historical memory and the symbolism of ancient traditions. The Mishnah (*Pesachim* 10) describes a seder with many of the elements found in our contemporary ritual. The *kiddush*, Four Questions, Exodus story, symbolic interpretations, Hallel psalms, and other prayers are all mentioned as part of the seder celebration of 1,900 years ago.

The format for the seder was derived from the Hellenistic talk-feast of the first century C.E. During that period, it was widespread practice to hold great banquets, with philosophic discussions as part of the meal. The rabbis substituted the *haggadah* for the philosophic discourse but retained many other elements of this Greco-Roman custom.

The seder ritual continued to grow and expand, but its essential features were established by the end of the first century.

4. When do we hold the seder?

The seder is held on the eve of the fifteenth day of Nisan in the Hebrew calendar, which may fall in March or April of the secular year. Reform Jews and Jews in Israel may have one or two seders. Traditional Jews outside of Israel usually hold seders on each of the first two nights of Pesach.

5. Where should the seder be held?

It is customary to conduct the first seder in the home with family, relatives, and friends. In recent years, many congregations have begun to hold community seders at the temple on the second night of Pesach for the entire congregation. There is, however, no rigidly prescribed location for the seder.

6. May we hold more than two seders?

Yes. There is no maximum. As a result, congregations, Jewish organizations, and interfaith groups often conduct seders on other nights of the festival. These seders serve as an additional source of inspiration, learning, and understanding for participants.

The order of the seder is contained in a special book called the *haggadah*.

The Haggadah

1. What does haggadah mean?

The Hebrew word *haggadah* means "telling" and refers to the special book containing the order of prayers, rituals, readings, and songs for the Pesach seder.

2. When did the haggadah originate?

Certain sections of the *haggadah* date back to the third century B.C.E. Most scholars, however, agree that the *haggadah*, as we know it today, originated some time after the destruction of the Second Temple in 70 C.E. It was then that the seder came into being as well. The *haggadah* fulfills the biblical injunction in Exodus 13:8: "And you shall tell (*vehigadeta*) your son on that day, saying: 'It is because of that which the Lord did for me when I came forth out of Egypt.'" The preserva-

tion of historical memory and timeless Jewish values remains the *haggadah's* foremost purpose.

3. Who wrote the first haggadah?

No one knows for certain. The many strands of Jewish writings contained within the *haggadah* make it more appropriate to speak of an "editor" rather than an "author." The great Rabban Gamliel II is mentioned in conjunction with the seder ritual which is recorded in the Mishnah (200 C.E.). Since we know that Gamliel arranged the order of the daily prayer service, many scholars hypothesize that he was also responsible for ordering the ancient seder.

4. When did the haggadah first appear in book form?

The earliest versions of the *haggadah* were appended to the prayer book. Rav Amram Gaon (ninth century) and Saadia Gaon (tenth century) and the great commentator Rashi were among those whose *siddurim* included *haggadot*.

It was not until the thirteenth century that the *haggadah* appeared as a separate volume. The first printed *haggadah* was published in Spain in 1482. Since that time, thousands of different editions of the *haggadah* have come into print in every country where Jews have lived and celebrated Pesach.

5. Why is it that the haggadah is illustrated, while the Torah and the siddur are not?

Traditional Jews never illustrated the Torah or the prayer book because they felt that the second of the Ten Commandments ("you shall not make any graven images") precluded such artistic expression. This was not the case with the *haggadah*. Beginning in the thirteenth century, beautifully illustrated and illuminated *haggadot* appeared in Jewish communities throughout the world. The *Darmstadt Haggadah* (fifteenth century) and the *Sarajevo Haggadah* (fourteenth century) are two of the best known examples.

The *CCAR Haggadah*, richly illustrated by Leonard Baskin, is one of the latest products of a historical tradition dating back over 600 years.

6. When did the first American Reform Jewish haggadah appear?

Interestingly, the history of the Reform *haggadah* parallels that of the traditional *haggadah*. Just as the first *haggadot* were appended to *siddurim*, so the first version of the *Union Prayer Book* (1892) contained a *haggadah* edited by S. I. Moses. The first *Union Haggadah*, appearing as a separate volume, was not issued until 1907. The 1907 edition was revised and reissued in 1923. The *CCAR Haggadah*, edited by Rabbi Herbert Bronstein, was first published in 1974.

The history of the *haggadah* is a fascinating one. Even today, new editions appear almost every year. Israeli kibbutz *haggadot*, *haggadot* with social action themes, traditional *haggadot* illustrated by prominent artists of our own times—all serve to "tell the story" of a people who believe in justice and freedom for all humanity.

Pesach: Some Little-Known Facts

Did You Know:

1. The number "four" pervades the seder.

Strangely, for a variety of historical reasons, circumstances have led to a large number of "fours" in the seder service. There are four questions, four sons, four mothers of Israel, four cups of wine, four special Pesach symbols, and four promises of redemption.

2. There were originally only three of the four questions we use today.

Today, the chanting of the Four Questions by the youngest child present is one of the most popular seder elements, but the original Mishnaic account of the four questions (200 C.E.) lists only

three of those we use today. One of the original four was dropped, since it referred to the Temple paschal sacrifice, and another question was substituted.

3. The Ballad of the Four Children is biblically based.

In four separate passages, the Torah reminds parents of their responsibility to tell their children the story of the Exodus. The Ballad of the Four Children grew out of these four injunctions. The questions asked by each of the children are found in the Torah (Exodus 12:26, 13:8, 13:14; Deuteronomy 6:20). The answers to the queries were formulated in later centuries.

4. Moses is mentioned only once in the traditional haggadah and not at all in the CCAR Haggadah.

It would be logical to expect the *haggadah* to

dwell at length on the life of Moses. After all, it was Moses who challenged Pharaoh face-to-face, who led the Israelites out of Egypt, and who brought them to Sinai. Yet the traditional *haggadah* refers to Moses only once, in a verse quoted from Scripture, and the *CCAR Haggadah* omits Moses altogether. Why?

The ancient rabbis feared that Moses might become deified as a result of his great leadership role. Moreover, they wanted to emphasize that God was responsible for Israel's redemption, acting in history with the assistance of God's inspired leaders. Moses, therefore, became a secondary figure in the *haggadah*, a custom that has endured to present times. In addition, the Book of Deuteronomy records that Moses' burial place is unknown for the same reason.

There is only one God in Judaism. And no person, however great, is accorded equal stature.

5. Elijah's cup originally resolved a rabbinic dispute.

We now know that the ceremony of opening the door for Elijah symbolizes our hope and belief in the coming of the Messianic Age. Traditional Jews believe that Elijah will appear as the forerunner of the Messiah. But the use of a fifth cup of wine poured for Elijah only began in the eighteenth century.

During the Middle Ages, a controversy arose over whether to have four or five cups of wine. As we have already seen, the four cups symbolized God's four promises of redemption to the Israelites as found in the Torah. Actually, however, there are five promises, which led some of the rabbis to advocate an additional cup of wine.

The debate could not be resolved, so the rabbis utilized a talmudic solution. In the Talmud, whenever an impasse occurred, the rabbis would say *teku*. We cannot decide. When Elijah comes, *he* will decide. The fifth cup of wine was thus instituted until such time as Elijah would come and make the final decision. Hence the name, Elijah's cup.

6. The afikoman was used as a good luck charm during the Middle Ages.

What Jewish child has not searched for the *afikoman* and been rewarded for finding it in some

secret hiding place? The *afikoman*, which means "dessert," is the traditional conclusion of the seder meal, after which no food is to be eaten.

Somehow, during the Middle Ages, mystical powers were ascribed to the *afikoman*. Some Jews took a piece of the *afikoman* with them on long ocean voyages, believing that it could prevent violent storms. Other Jews hung part of the *afikoman* in their homes to ward off demons. It is not clear how these superstitions arose, but in those times they were central to many Jewish communities.

7. No women are mentioned by name in the traditional haggadah.

No woman's name appears in the *haggadah*, but many of the *haggadah*'s illustrations include women. The *CCAR Haggadah*, for example, portrays the four mothers of Israel (Sarah, Rebeccah, Leah, and Rachel) most beautifully. Why the apparent contradiction?

In ancient times, only men attended the seder. Indeed, the language of the *haggadah* indicates that it was intended for fathers to relate to their sons. It was only later that the seder became a family event and much later (thirteenth through fourteenth centuries) that illustrated *haggadot* began to appear. The illustrators reflected contemporary Pesach ritual, and thus their pictures captured the emerging participative role of women in the seder.

8. Familiar songs of Pesach were not part of the early seder.

The joyful melodies of Pesach are an indispensable part of the seder today. Yet these songs were much later additions to the *haggadah*. *Addir Hu* ("God of Might") did not appear until the fourteenth century in the *Darmstadt Haggadah*. *Chad Gadya* ("An Only Kid") and *Echad Mi Yodea?* ("Who Knows One?") were included for the first time in the *Prague Haggadah* of 1590.

Whatever their origins, the elements of the seder have evolved into a powerful symbol system, rich in Jewish values and teachings, for Jews of all ages. The product of centuries of development enables us, as modern Jews, to "tell the story" in joy, gladness, and with eternal hope.

·4·

CHANUKAH

Some Historical Background

1. What does Chanukah mean?

The Hebrew word Chanukah means "dedication" and refers to the joyous eight-day celebration through which Jews commemorate the victory of the Maccabees over the armies of Syria in 165 B.C.E. and the subsequent liberation and "rededication" of the Temple in Jerusalem.

2. Is Chanukah biblically based?

No. Unlike most Jewish holidays, Chanukah is not mentioned in the Torah, Prophets, or Writings. The historical events upon which the celebration is based are recorded in I and II Maccabees, two books contained within a later collection of writings known as the Apocrypha.

3. What is the Apocrypha?

When the final format of the Bible was debated (first century C.E.), a number of books were considered for inclusion but ultimately rejected. The two books of Maccabees were among those passed over. Some time later, because of the popularity which some of the rejected writings enjoyed among the people, fourteen of them were gathered into a single collection called the Apocrypha. The term Apocrypha comes from a Greek word mean-

ing "hidden writing." While the apocryphal works were never made part of the Hebrew Bible, they were included in the Greek and Latin versions.

4. If the story of Chanukah was so obscure, how did the holiday become so popular?

Technically, Chanukah is considered a "minor" Jewish festival. Yet it ranks along with Pesach and Purim as one of the most beloved Jewish family holidays. Clearly, the stirring story associated with Chanukah, the rituals which emerged from it, and the special Chanukah games and foods combined to capture the Jewish imagination and elevate its status within the Jewish community.

5. What is the story of Chanukah?

In the year 168 B.C.E., the Syrian tyrant Antiochus Epiphanes sent his soldiers to Jerusalem. The Syrians desecrated the Temple, and Antiochus declared that Judaism was to be abolished. The only options he offered Jews were conversion or death. Altars and idols were set up throughout Judea for the purpose of worshiping Greek gods. Antiochus outlawed the observance of Shabbat, the festivals, and circumcision.

On the twenty-fifth day of the Hebrew month of Kislev in 168 B.C.E., the Temple was renamed for the Greek god Zeus. Pigs were sacrificed in the Temple. The Torah was splattered with pigs'

Furious, Antiochus decided to destroy the people of Judea. He sent a large army, with instructions to kill every man, woman, and child. Though outnumbered, Judah Maccabee and his fighters miraculously won two major battles, routing the Syrians decisively. By 165 B.C.E., the terror of Antiochus had ended. The Jews had won a victory for their land and their faith.

The idols were torn down, and, on the morning of the twenty-fifth day of Kislev in 165 B.C.E., the Temple in Jerusalem was reconsecrated—three years to the day after its original defilement. In celebration, the people of Jerusalem lit bright lights in front of their homes and decided to mark their deliverance with an annual eight-day festival. It was called the Feast of Lights, the Feast of Dedication, or simply Chanukah.

6. Is that why we celebrate Chanukah for eight days? What about the jar of oil that burned for eight days?

Originally, the eight-day Feast of Lights was intended to parallel the eight days of Sukot. The books of the Maccabees made no mention of the beautiful legend concerning the jar of oil which has come to be a part of Chanukah. Several centuries later (500 C.E.), the story of the cruse of oil emerged in the Talmud.

The legend relates that, when the Maccabees entered the Temple and began to cleanse it, they immediately relit the *ner tamid,* or Eternal Light. A single jar of oil remained, which was sufficient for only one day. The messenger who was sent to secure additional oil took eight days to complete his mission. But, miraculously, the single cruse of oil continued to burn for eight days. The rabbis of the Talmud, therefore, attributed the eight days of Chanukah to the miracle of the little jar of oil.

We continue the ancient customs related to Chanukah today, commemorating the liberation of our people and their affirmation of human dignity and freedom of religion. In Jewish homes throughout the world, the eve of the twenty-fifth of Kislev begins an eight-day celebration involving many joyous customs and ceremonies.

blood and then burned. Thousands of Jews chose to die rather than commit idolatry. Among these martyrs was a woman named Hannah who, with her seven sons, defied the Syrian decree.

But slowly a resistance movement developed against the cruelty of Antiochus, led by a priestly family known as the Hasmoneans, or Maccabees. The head of the family was an elderly man named Mattathias. He and his five sons left Jerusalem and took up residence in a small town north of Jerusalem, called Modi'in. When Syrian soldiers appeared in the town and commanded the inhabitants to offer sacrifices to Zeus, Mattathias and his sons refused. Mattathias killed one Jew who began to sacrifice to Zeus, and his sons then turned upon the Syrian troops and slew them.

It was a turning point in the struggle. The Maccabees became instant folk heroes. Fleeing to the hills with their followers, they conducted a campaign of guerilla warfare against the occupying Syrian forces. Mattathias's son, Judah, known as "The Hammer," became the chief strategist and military leader.

Chanukah: Ceremonies, Symbols, Customs

The modern home celebration of Chanukah centers around the lighting of Chanukah candles in the menorah, unique foods, and special games and songs.

1. What is the meaning of menorah?

Menorah is a Hebrew word meaning "candelabrum." In relation to Chanukah, it refers to the nine-branched ceremonial lamp in which the Chanukah candles are placed and then blessed.

2. Is the menorah unique to Chanukah?

No. The menorah originated as a religious symbol in biblical times. The Torah records how the great artist Bezalel fashioned a seven-branched menorah for the desert tabernacle in fulfillment of a Divine commandment (Exodus 25:31–40; 37:17–24). Such a seven-branched menorah adorned the Temple in Jerusalem and was carried away by the Roman legions at the time of its destruction in 70 C.E. While the Roman Empire has long since vanished, a seven-branched menorah stands before the Knesset building in Israel, yet another tangible reminder of the indestructibility of the Jewish people.

3. How did the Chanukah menorah originate?

The nine-branched Chanukah menorah was a modification of the biblical model and seems to have originated in the first century C.E. It had eight branches, one for each day of the holiday, and a ninth branch for the *shamash* or "servant" light.

In ancient times, oil was used in the menorah. Over time, candles were substituted for the oil.

Interestingly, some scholars believe that the use of small candles for the menorah was a deliberate choice, designed to distinguish Chanukah lights from Christian votive candles. Except in times of religious persecution, the menorah was placed outside the front door or, as is the custom today, displayed in the window of every Jewish home.

4. How do we light the Chanukah candles?

In a celebrated talmudic dispute, two great Jewish teachers, Hillel and Shammai, argued whether we should begin by lighting eight candles and gradually decrease to one (Shammai), or begin with one candle and add an additional one each night, thus continuously increasing the light and joy of the holiday (Hillel). The majority ruled with Hillel. Thus, on the first night of Chanukah, we recite or chant the blessings and light one candle with the *shamash*, two on the second night, and so on. Customarily, the candles are placed in the menorah from right to left but lit from left to right.

5. What are the Chanukah candle blessings?

There are two *berachot* which are chanted or recited on every night of Chanukah. The first is a blessing over the candles themselves: *Baruch Atah Adonai Elohenu Melech ha'olam asher kideshanu bemitzvotav vetzivanu lehadlik ner shel Chanukah.* "Blessed are You, O Lord our God, Ruler of the world, who has sanctified us through your *mitzvot* and commanded us to kindle the Chanukah lights."

The second *berachah* expresses thanks for the "miracle" of deliverance: *Baruch Atah Adonai Elohenu Melech ha'olam she'asah nisim laavotenu bayamim hahem bazeman hazeh.* "Blessed are You, O Lord our God, Ruler of the world, who did wondrous things for our ancestors in former times at this season."

There is a third *berachah* which is chanted or recited only on the first night. This is the *Shehecheyanu* prayer, pronounced by Jews on all happy occasions: *Baruch Atah Adonai Elohenu Melech ha'olam shehecheyanu vekiyemanu vehigiyanu lazeman hazeh.* "Blessed are You, O Lord our God, Ruler of the world, who has kept us in life, sustained us, and brought us to this happy time."

Any member or members of the family may chant or recite the blessings. One person lights and holds the *shamash*, the *berachot* are pronounced, and the candles are then lit. On Shabbat, the Chanukah candles are lit before the Shabbat candles. The traditional melody for the Chanukah candle blessings may be found in "Chanukah Candle Blessings," arranged by David J. Putterman, published by Transcontinental Music (UAHC catalogue #990439, $1.50).

6. How did the game of dreidel come to be associated with Chanukah?

Dreidel is a derivative of a German word meaning "top," and the game is an adaptation of an old German gambling game. Chanukah was one of the few times of the year when the rabbis permitted games of chance. The dreidel, therefore, was a natural candidate for Chanukah entertainment.

The four sides of the top bear four Hebrew letters: *nun*, *gimel*, *hei*, and *shin*. Players would begin by "anteing" a certain number of coins, nuts, or other objects. Each one in turn would then spin the dreidel and proceed as follows: *nun* ("nichts")—take nothing; *gimel* ("ganz")—take everything; *hei* ("halb")—take half; *shin* ("shtell")—put in.

The winner would often receive money (Chanukah *gelt*). Over time, the gambling terms were reinterpreted to stand for the Hebrew phrase *Nes Gadol Hayah Sham*, "A great miracle happened there." Thus, even an ordinary game of chance was invested with Jewish values and served to remind Jews of the important message of Chanukah. Today, Jewish children throughout the world continue to enjoy the game of dreidel. In Israel, one letter on the dreidel has been changed. The *shin* has been replaced with a *pei*, transforming the Hebrew phrase into *Nes Gadol Hayah Po*, "A great miracle happened *here*."

7. Why do we eat latkes on Chanukah?

A common explanation is that we eat latkes (potato pancakes) because they are cooked in oil and thus remind us of the miracle of the single cruse.

Rabbi Solomon Freehof, a great contemporary Jewish scholar, has hypothesized that the eating of latkes may have grown out of an old custom of eating *milchig* (dairy) foods on Chanukah. *Milchig* foods evolved into *milchig* pancakes and then into latkes, possibly because the main potato crop became available about the time of Chanukah.

No one knows for certain how the association began, but for anyone who feasts on latkes at Chanukah time, a historical rationale is unnecessary.

8. Why do we give gifts on Chanukah?

Again, no one knows for sure. Many scholars postulate that the practice is a carry-over from the biblically-based custom of sending gifts (*mishloach manot*) to one's friends on Purim. It is clear, however, that presents were never a major element in Chanukah, which emphasizes enduring religious and ethical values.

9. Who wrote "Rock of Ages"?

Ma'oz Tzur, or "Rock of Ages," was composed in Europe in the twelfth or thirteenth century by a man known as Mordecai. His words were set to different melodies over the centuries.

When all is said and done, perhaps the most important message of Chanukah may be found in the name of the holiday itself—Dedication. When Jews have dedicated themselves, through faith and action, to the pursuit of high religious and human ideals, Judaism has been strong. That imperative, to strengthen our religion and our people, remains an important challenge at this season, in every generation.

·5·

PURIM

The Story and the Message

The Talmud declares: "When Adar arrives, our joy increases." And rightfully so. For the fourteenth day of the Hebrew month of Adar marks the holiday of Purim, the paradigm of Jewish deliverance from cruel tyranny. The characters of King Ahashuerus, Queen Vashti, Mordechai, Esther, and the evil Haman parade before us, vivid reminders of our people's will and capacity to survive.

1. What is the meaning of Purim?

The Hebrew word *purim* derives from the old Persian word "pur," meaning "lots." It refers to the "lottery tickets" used by Haman to determine a date for his planned destruction of the Jews of Persia.

2. Where is the story of Purim found?

The story of Purim is contained in the Scroll of Esther, Megillat Esther. There are four other biblical *megillot*, each read in the synagogue on a holiday compatible with its theme. Esther is read on Purim, Ruth on Shavuot, Lamentations on Tishah Be'av, Ecclesiastes on Sukot, and Song of Songs on Pesach. Only in the case of Purim, however, does the *megillah* relate the holiday's basic story.

3. What is the story of Purim?

King Ahashuerus, great ruler of Persia, once gave a banquet for his subjects. When Queen Vashti refused to entertain the guests, she lost her crown (and possibly her head as well).

A beauty contest was held to select Vashti's successor. The winner was a Jewish woman, Hadassah, whose Persian name was Esther. Brought to the king's court by her uncle Mordechai, she became the new queen.

It was Mordechai's custom to sit at the gate by the palace. One day he overheard two men, Bigthan and Teresh, planning to kill the king. He reported it to Esther and the plot was foiled, but the king was not made aware of what Mordechai had done for him.

About the same time, Ahashuerus made Haman the Agagite prime minister of Persia. This was a position of great power, and all who saw Haman were supposed to bow down before him. When Haman passed by the gate to the palace, however, Mordechai refused to bow, since Jews pay homage only to God. Haman was furious and decided to destroy all the Jews of Persia in revenge. He drew lots (*purim*) to fix the date, then convinced the king, through bribery and anti-Semitic slander, to sanction his evil plan.

Mordechai told Esther of the decree, and she decided to go directly to Ahashuerus to save her people. This was very dangerous, for anyone who went to the king without being summoned faced immediate execution. Still, Esther went and invited the king and Haman to a dinner which she would prepare. Both the king and Haman accepted.

That night, the king could not sleep, so he had one of his servants read to him from the book which chronicled the events of the kingdom. For the first time, Ahashuerus learned about the assassination which Mordechai had thwarted and decided to reward him. Haman was asked how a man whom the king wished to reward might be honored. The prime minister imagined that *he* was to be honored and thus described an elaborate parade in which the man, dressed in royal robes, would be led through the city on horseback. The king was thrilled with the idea and commanded Haman to lead Mordechai through the city in just such a procession.

Haman angrily carried out the king's order and arrived at Esther's dinner party more determined than ever to exterminate the Jews. But it was not to be. Esther revealed that she was Jewish, that Haman planned to destroy her people, and begged Ahashuerus to reverse the order of genocide.

It was too late to cancel the edict. Too many Persians were already preparing to attack Jewish communities. But a new decree went out, empowering the Jews and their friends to fight and defend themselves.

Haman was hanged on the gallows he had prepared for Mordechai. Mordechai was named the new prime minister. The Jews defeated their attackers and were saved. And the fourteenth of Adar was set aside as a day of feasting and joy, a time for giving gifts to friends and charity to the poor, a time for remembering how the Jewish people had resisted and defeated a villain who sought their annihilation.

4. Is the story of Esther true?

Most probably not, though there is a supposed ancient tomb of Esther and Mordechai in Iran. Some scholars hypothesize that Ahashuerus was either Xerxes I, who ruled Persia from 486–465 B.C.E., or Artaxerxes II, king from 404–359 B.C.E. But historical records of the period make no mention of Haman, Esther, or Mordechai, nor do they refer to any of the incidents in the Scroll of Esther.

There are many theories as to how the Book of Esther came to be written. Some scholars hold that Purim coopted and "Judaized" the popular pagan carnivals of that era. Jewish leaders could not stop the people from feasting and parading, so they validated the practice in a Jewish historical framework, in the Scroll of Esther.

The second theory affirms that Esther was written about the time of the Maccabean revolt (165 B.C.E.). In the flush of victory, say these scholars, the book was created to reinforce the national mood of confidence in deliverance.

A third hypothesis is perhaps the most interesting. The Babylonians had a New Year celebration when they believed their gods Marduk and Ishtar cast lots to determine each individual's fate. Then, say these scholars, the elements of this pagan festival were borrowed, rewritten, and transformed into Purim, with Marduk becoming Mordechai, Ishtar becoming Esther, and lots (*purim*) playing a pivotal role in the plot.

No one theory is universally accepted, however, and the real origins of Megillat Esther remain a mystery.

5. But how can a Jewish holiday be based on an event which may never have happened?

Purim is unusual in many respects. First, it has many secular aspects. Indeed, Esther is the only Book of the Bible in which God is not mentioned. Second, Purim, like Chanukah, is viewed by tradition as a minor festival.

The elevation of Purim to a major holiday in the eyes of the Jewish people was a result of the Jewish historical experience. Over the centuries, Haman became the embodiment of every anti-Semite in every land where Jews were oppressed. Jewish communities throughout the world, when delivered from tragedy, often wrote their own *megillot* and celebrated local Purims. The emotional power of the holiday increased in every generation, moving one anonymous ancient Jewish writer to remark: "When all the other books of the prophets and writings are forgotten, the Book of Esther

will be remembered." Even the enemies of the Jews recognized *their* identification with Haman. In an eerie prophecy, in 1944, Adolf Hitler declared that, if the Nazis lost the war, the Jews would celebrate a second Purim.

The significance of Purim, then, lies not in how it began, but in what it has become—a thankful and joyous affirmation of Jewish survival against all odds.

Purim: The Celebration

Purim is truly unique. How else might we explain a holiday whose message and power have endured for over 2,000 years—despite the fact that its story (Megillat Esther) probably never took place!

The special quality of Purim is also reflected in the intriguing customs associated with both its synagogue and home celebration. "Blotting out" Haman's name, the greggar, masquerading, *mishloach manot,* Purim spiels, and becoming slightly inebriated are all part of the rich and colorful tradition of this holiday of deliverance.

1. Why do we make noise when Haman's name is read from the Megillah?

Every Jew has, at one time or another, yelled, screamed, sounded the greggar, or banged a pot or pan at the mention of Haman's name. The custom has fascinating biblical origins.

Exodus 17 describes a bitter battle in the wilderness between the Israelites and the soldiers of King Amalek. Although Israel prevails, the Torah records God "saying" to Moses: "Write this for a memorial in the book . . . I will utterly blot out the remembrance of Amalek from under the

heavens" (Exodus 17:14). In Deuteronomy 25:19, this curse on Amalek is repeated: ". . . You shall blot out the remembrance of Amalek from under heaven; you shall not forget." The sense of the passage is clear. God is telling the children of Israel that the descendants of Amalek will always be their enemies and thus to "blot them out."

Indeed, history proved that to be true. Many years later, Agag, then king of Amalek, became a bitter foe of the Jewish people, a slaughterer of women and children. In fact, King Saul was dethroned for sparing Agag's life after Israel's military victory over the Amalekites. The prophet Samuel executed Agag, and the name of Amalek was "blotted out."

Now, turning to Esther 3:1, we see that Haman is identified as "the son of Hammedatha the Agagite," in short, a direct descendant of Amalek! It is reasonable to assume that the author of Esther deliberately forged a bond between Amalek and Haman so as to accentuate Haman's evil character. Remembering the ancient injunction to "blot out" Amalek's name, the Jews proceeded to do just that—not by violence, but through noise. The custom of "blotting out" the name of Haman was thus born and endures today.

2. Where did the greggar originate?

Greggar comes from a Polish word meaning "rattle." Beginning about the thirteenth century, Jews throughout Europe sounded the greggar whenever the *megillah* mentioned evil Haman.

The greggar was by no means, however, the only way in which the congregation expressed its glee at Haman's downfall. Jews of talmudic times burned Haman in effigy, a custom which continued in some countries well into the nineteenth century. Thirteenth-century European Jews drew Haman's picture or wrote his name on stones which they banged together. Others wrote his name on the soles of their shoes and stamped them on the ground. Still others would write Haman's name on a slip of paper and erase it!

These seemingly unusual activities all had great symbolic value for the Jewish community. Haman stood for every tyrant, every dictator who had tried to destroy the Jews. Purim customs such as these served to declare: "We are still alive! We endure! We will not disappear! We are the Jewish people!"

3. Why do we wear costumes on Purim?

Purim borrowed freely from the pagan carnivals of ancient times, especially from the later Roman carnivals. Beginning about the fifteenth century,

European Jews adapted the gala costumes and processions of these carnivals for Purim. Dressed in colorful masks and attire, children would march through the town, with tiny Mordechais, Esthers, and Hamans, parading in joy from street to street.

Most congregations today carry on that custom through Purim carnivals, costume contests, and other similar events. Children in the State of Israel celebrate Purim in grand fashion. If you're ever in Tel Aviv on Purim day, you'll see hundreds of beautifully costumed youngsters in a display of Jewish self-affirmation that is impossible to forget.

4. How did Purim spiels start?

Purim plays, or Purim spiels, originated about the fifteenth century in Germany. Some of these slapstick spoofs became classics in the communities where they were first performed, and many of the original manuscripts have been preserved. But Jews of today write their own scripts, which are just as humorous and enjoyable as creations of the past.

5. Are you really supposed to get drunk on Purim?

According to the Talmud, yes. The exact quotation is: "On Purim, one should drink until he can no longer tell the difference between 'cursed be Haman' and 'blessed be Mordechai' " (*Megillah* 7b).

This runs counter to normative Jewish teachings which generally condemn intoxication as unseemly. But Purim was exempted from the usual rules. The custom of allowing excessive drinking was probably a result of Purim's biblical status as a *mishteh* (literally, "feast" but also meaning "drink"). The rabbis monitored the seeming permissiveness carefully, but, so long as individuals did not become abusive or destructive, Purim was a time when almost anything was permitted.

6. Why do we eat Hamantashen on Purim?

Hamantashen originated in Europe. The term

derives from two German words, "mohn" (poppy seed) and "taschen" (pockets). The association with Purim was solidified by substituting the name of Haman for "mohn." Some hold that the Hamantashen symbolize the three-cornered hat which Haman wore.

Actually, there are many foods which came to be associated with Purim, but Hamantashen emerged as the most popular delicacy. The three-cornered pastry, filled with poppy seeds, apricots, or prunes, has become an essential element in Purim's joy.

7. Why do we send gifts and give charity on Purim?

The Book of Esther 9:22 enjoins the Jews to "make days of feasting and gladness, and of sending gifts to one another (*mishloach manot*), and gifts to the poor." It is typical of Judaism that, even during a holiday of revelry, we remember others, especially those less fortunate than ourselves. It is customary to send two gifts to at least one friend and to give a single gift to at least two poor people. Even the poorest Jew is expected to share with others. Thus we learn that *tzedakah*, at all times and in all places, is a religious duty.

8. Esther's Hebrew name was Hadassah. Is there any connection between her and the great women's organization of today?

Yes. After a visit to Palestine, the great Jewish leader Henrietta Szold decided to form a Zionist organization for women. She envisioned this group working for the health of women and children in what was to become the modern State of Israel.

The founding meeting was held at Congregation Emanu-El of New York on Purim, 1912. The women constituted themselves as the Hadassah chapter of the Daughters of Zion. Eventually, the name became Hadassah. The legendary biblical woman, who centuries before had delivered her people, thus gave her name to a new generation of women who would seek to emulate her noble example.

Some would call this coincidence. Perhaps. But we Jews have learned to expect such "accidents"— an Abraham, a Moses, an Esther, a Henrietta Szold, a Herzl—all appearing at exactly the right moment in our history. Purim teaches us that history can be capricious. But, while others may seek to determine our fate by "lots," it will ultimately be Jewish strength, commitment, and faith which ensure a bright future for our people.

·6·

ROSH HASHANAH

An Unusual New Year

As fall approaches, Jews throughout the world begin to prepare for a unique ten-day period of prayer, self-examination, fasting, and repentance. It is time for the *Yamin Noraim*, the Days of Awe, the High Holy Days: Rosh Hashanah and Yom Kippur.

1. What is the meaning of Rosh Hashanah?

Rosh Hashanah (literally, "Head of the Year") refers to the Jewish New Year celebration initiating the High Holy Days.

2. When do we celebrate Rosh Hashanah?

We observe Rosh Hashanah on the first day of the Hebrew month of Tishrei. This may fall in either September or October of the secular year, due to the differences between the solar and lunar calendars. Most Reform Jews celebrate one day of the holiday, while Conservative, Orthodox, and Israeli Jews observe two days.

3. Is Rosh Hashanah biblically based?

In a sense it is. The Book of Leviticus (23:24–25) declares: "In the seventh month, on the first day of the month, you shall observe a day of rest, a memorial proclaimed with the blowing of the shofar, a holy convocation." This day eventually became Rosh Hashanah, the Jewish New Year. But it was not known as such at that time.

4. How could the first day of the seventh month become the new year?

In ancient times, there were four "new years" in the Jewish calendar. Each one had a distinct significance:

   a. The first of Nisan: the New Year of Kings, a date used to calculate the number of years a given king had reigned.
   b. The first of Elul: the new year for tithing of cattle, a time when one out of every ten cattle was marked and offered as a sacrifice to God.
   c. The first of Tishrei: the agricultural new year, the New Year of the Years.
   d. The fifteenth of Shevat: Tu Bishvat, the New Year of the Trees.

The Torah refers to Nisan as the first month of the Jewish year. Despite this, however, the first of Tishrei emerged as what we now know as Rosh Hashanah.

5. How did this happen?

A number of powerful forces converged, resulting in this decision. To begin with, the Babylonians marked a "Day of Judgment." The Babylonians believed that, on that day, a convocation of their deities assembled in the temple of the god Marduk. These gods, they held, renewed the world and judged each human being, inscribing the fate of every individual on a tablet of destiny.

The legend was a powerful one, and Jews living

among the Babylonians most likely borrowed elements from it in shaping Rosh Hashanah. The meeting of many deities evolved into a belief that the one God judged every Jew on that day, with the completely righteous immediately inscribed in the Book of Life and the completely wicked consigned to a sad fate. Those "in between," however, had ten days, concluding on Yom Kippur, in which to repent before the books were sealed for another year.

In addition to the biblical "holy convocation" and the transformed Babylonian "Day of Judgment," the first of Tishrei was associated with the anniversary of the creation of the world, *Yom Harat Olam*. For these three compelling reasons, the first day of the seventh month ultimately became the "official" Jewish New Year.

6. When did the holiday get the name Rosh Hashanah?

It was not until about the second century C.E.

The name Rosh Hashanah first occurs in the Mishnah. Before then, however, the day had many other designations. The oldest name, found in the Torah (Numbers 29:1), is *Yom Teruah* (Day of Sounding the Shofar). Two other names, undoubtedly reflecting Babylonian influence, were *Yom Hazikaron* (Day of Remembrance) and *Yom Hadin* (Day of Judgment). While those terms are still preserved in the liturgy and rabbinic literature, Jews all over the world today usually refer to Rosh Hashanah as the Jewish New Year.

7. Is Rosh Hashanah like the secular new year?

While there are common elements of joy and celebration, Rosh Hashanah is far more than an evening of parties and entertainment. It is a deeply religious occasion, ushering in a period of profound spiritual significance. The customs and symbols of Rosh Hashanah reflect the holiday's dual emphasis, happiness and humility.

Rosh Hashanah: Customs and Symbols

We now know the origins of Rosh Hashanah and how it came to be the Jewish New Year. But there are a number of fascinating customs and symbols associated with the holiday which also deserve our careful attention.

1. What is the meaning of Selichot?

Selichot, a Hebrew word meaning "forgiveness," refers to the special penitential prayers recited by Jews during the Rosh Hashanah season. The *Selichot* liturgy contains some of the finest Jewish religious poetry ever composed.

Traditional Jews recite *Selichot* beginning late at night on the Saturday before Rosh Hashanah and continue before dawn on the days between the New Year and Yom Kippur. Reform congregations that observe *Selichot* usually do so on the

Blowing the Shofar on New-Year's Day.
(From a Passover Haggadah, Amsterdam, 1695.)

Saturday night just prior to Rosh Hashanah, a solemn and fitting preparation for ten days of reflection and self-examination.

2. Are there any special home rituals for Rosh Hashanah?

Yes. On the eve of the holiday, we recite the festival candle blessing and *kiddush*. We pronounce the *Motzi* prayer as usual, but traditionally over a round *chalah*. Finally, just before beginning the Rosh Hashanah meal, we customarily eat *chalah* or apples dipped in honey.

3. What is the festival candle blessing?

The candles are lit first, as on Shabbat, and we then pronounce the *berachah: Baruch Atah Adonai Elohenu Melech ha'olam asher kideshanu bemitzvotav vetzivanu lehadlik ner shel (Shabbat veshel) yom tov.*

4. Where can we find the festival kiddush?

The festival *kiddush*, Hebrew and English, can be found in "The *Kiddush* through the Year," arranged by Herbert Fromm, published by Transcontinental Music (UAHC catalogue #990776, $3.50).

5. Why do we use a round chalah?

There are many explanations for this custom. Some people see the round shape as reflecting the continuing cycle of years and seasons. The most common interpretation, however, is that the *chalah* resembles a crown, thus symbolizing the kingship of God. At a time of year when our thoughts turn to repentance and resolutions of self-improvement, the round *chalah* reminds the Jew that God is central to our people and to our faith.

6. Why do we eat apples and honey?

Over the centuries, Jews have dipped *chalah*, apples, grapes, and other fruits in honey, eating them on Rosh Hashanah while wishing one another a "sweet" New Year. Apples, however, are most commonly used.

Why apples? Why not pears or oranges? No one knows for sure, but there are some interesting possibilities. Scholars of ancient cultures tell us that mystical powers were once ascribed to the apple. People ate the fruit in the belief that it could guarantee good health and personal well-being. There are also a number of oddities in-

volving the apple which defy explanation. For example, although the story of Adam and Eve does not specify which "forbidden fruit" was eaten, we customarily speak of the apple as the cause of expulsion from paradise. Why do we say "an apple a day keeps the doctor away"? Why did school children once bring an apple for the teacher?

If one assumes that customs in society arise for a reason, then the scholars are probably correct in theorizing that the apple was once invested with great symbolic significance. Whether the custom of eating apples and honey arose out of superstition, ties to the Genesis account, or for some other reason, it is a lovely—and delicious—way for families to begin a New Year together.

7. What is the origin of the Rosh Hashanah greeting Leshanah Tovah Tikatevu?

This Hebrew phrase, which means "May you be inscribed for a good year," is very ancient. In all probability, the greeting initially reflected a strong superstitious belief.

We have already discussed the ancient legend (adapted from the Babylonians) of two books of destiny, opened by God on Rosh Hashanah and closed on Yom Kippur. Naturally, Jews hoped that their families and friends would enjoy a year of health, happiness, and success. *Leshanah Tovah Tikatevu* probably grew out of that spirit of well-wishing, as well as a belief that they could "help one another along" through its use.

Interestingly, it was considered an insult by many to greet friends with this phrase *after* the Rosh Hashanah service. Since the legend affirmed that the completely righteous were immediately inscribed in the Book of Life, use of *Leshanah Tovah Tikatevu* after the service implied that a friend or relative was still in need of repentance! Today, however, we use the greeting freely, an expression of fellowship and sincere good wishes for all Jews in our congregation and community.

8. Where did the shofar originate?

The shofar ("horn" or "trumpet") is one of the world's oldest wind instruments. It was important in Jewish history long before it became associated with the holiday we now know as Rosh Hash-

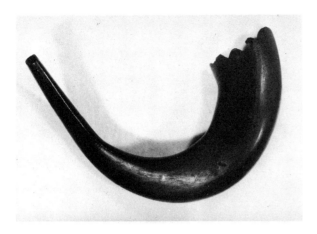

anah. Throughout the Bible, we find the shofar mentioned as a central element in ritual observance. For example, the shofar was sounded at the new moon and at solemn feasts. The Book of Exodus (19:16, 20:15) describes how the shofar was blown at Sinai to prepare the people for the giving of Torah. The Book of Joshua (6:1–20) details the use of the shofar as part of the conquest of Jericho. And, as we have seen, the celebration which ultimately evolved into Rosh Hashanah was originally called *Yom Teruah* (Day of Blowing the Shofar).

9. Why do we blow the shofar on Rosh Hashanah?

There are many explanations for this custom which has become such an integral part of the Jewish New Year. Certainly the link with *Yom Teruah* was an early reason, but there are many others.

Some people feel that the shofar reminds us of the Sinai experience. At a time when Jews are closest to God, they say, this historical moment is relived through the shofar service. The great Jewish philosopher Maimonides saw the sounding of the shofar as a call to repentance, while the Talmud viewed the ritual as a means of confusing Satan so that he would not harm the Jewish people during this time of judgment.

The most common explanation of the shofar in the Rosh Hashanah service, however, derives from the account of the binding of Isaac in Genesis 22, which we read on the New Year. As you recall, the sacrifice of Isaac was averted through the substitution of a ram for the boy. Although the key message is a statement against human sacrifice, the story also became a basis for blowing a ram's horn on Rosh Hashanah.

10. Is that the only reason we use a ram's horn?

No. Traditional Jews also avoided horns from a cow or ox because of the negative role that the golden calf played in undermining the Jewish people's faith at Sinai. In addition, the shofar is customarily curved, symbolic of the human heart bent in humble repentance on this important day.

·7·

YOM KIPPUR

1. What is the meaning of Yom Kippur?

Yom Kippur means "Day of Atonement" and refers to the annual Jewish observance of fasting, prayer, and repentance. Most Jews consider this day the holiest in the Jewish calendar.

2. When did Yom Kippur originate?

Yom Kippur dates from biblical times. In three separate passages in the Torah, the Jewish people are told that "the tenth day of the seventh month is the Day of Atonement. It shall be a sacred occasion for you: You shall practice self denial. . ." (Leviticus 23:27). That commandment became the basis of Yom Kippur as we know it today, which we observe on the tenth day of the Hebrew calendar month of Tishrei.

3. But isn't Tishrei the first month of the Jewish year? After all, Rosh Hashanah, the Jewish New Year, falls on the first day of Tishrei.

We have already learned that the ancient Israelites observed four new years. The biblical reference point for numbering months is always the new year of spring, the month of Nisan. In that framework, Tishrei would be the seventh month.

The tenth of Tishrei was seen as an appropriate Day of Atonement for another reason as well. You will recall that the incident of the golden calf led Moses to shatter the first tablets of the law (Exodus 32:19). According to legend, he re-

turned to Sinai, received a second set of tablets, then descended on the tenth of Tishrei to find the Jewish people fasting and repenting. The midrash relates that God then forgave the people and established that day as a day of atonement for all generations.

4. Does Yom Kippur have any other names?

Yes. The Torah refers to Yom Kippur as Shabbat Shabbaton, "a Sabbath of complete rest," while the Talmud denotes Yom Kippur simply as Yoma, "The Day." Interestingly, the Islamic religion once held the tenth of Tishrei as holy. According to Islam, this was the date when the Koran was sent from heaven. The day was designated the Fast of Ashurah and remained a solemn observance for many years among Islamic peoples.

5. How was Yom Kippur observed in ancient times?

The biblical ceremony of atonement, which reflected the strong belief in magic and superstition prevalent among peoples of that era, was quite different from that of today. The high priest of the Temple, or *kohen*, performed a rite of expiation on behalf of the entire people. Leviticus 16:7–22 describes this ritual. Two goats were brought before the *kohen*. One was sacrificed on the altar as a sin offering. The *kohen* then placed his hands on the head of the second goat and confessed

32·

over it all the sins of the people. The goat was driven off into the wilderness, supposedly carrying with it all the guilt that the Israelites had accumulated during the year. This primitive custom was the origin of the term "scapegoat," the projecting of blame for personal deeds upon another.

6. How did Yom Kippur evolve after the Temple was destroyed?

After the destruction of the First Temple (586 (B.C.E.), the Jewish people were driven into exile. There they felt a deep need to find some means for absolution of guilt. Prayer, fasting, and the giving of charity emerged as powerful means for attaining this spiritual release. Even after the Temple was rebuilt, these customs of repentance persevered. Thus, when the Second Temple fell (70 C.E.) and animal sacrifice was no longer possible, the seeds had already been sown for Yom Kippur as we know it today.

New rituals appeared. One of the most popular customs, arising in the first century C.E., was the ceremony of *kapparot*. This rite, probably derived from the biblical scapegoat ritual, involved whirling a chicken around one's head three times (a mystical number), then slaughtering the animal and giving the meat or money obtained for it to the poor. Men usually used a rooster for *kapparot*, while women used a hen. Fowl were used because of their ready availability. Here, as in the Torah, the assumption was that the sins of the individual were mystically transferred to the animal. Today, some Jews still observe this custom, and many preserve the practice of giving money to charity at this season.

7. Why do we fast on Yom Kippur?

Fasting was originally seen as fulfilling the biblical commandment to "practice self-denial." Midrashic writings also stress fasting as a historical reminder of Israel's repentance for the incident of the golden calf. More importantly, however, the Yom Kippur fast enables us, for at least one day each year, to ignore our physical desires and instead stress our spiritual needs. We concentrate on prayer, repentance, and self-improvement before returning to our usual daily routine.

8. Who has to fast?

According to tradition, all females from age twelve and all males from age thirteen must fast. It was and is the custom in many communities to encourage even younger children to begin fasting for several hours each year, so as to prepare them for full participation in the holiday when the proper time arrives. The traditional fast encompasses a full twenty-four-hour period, beginning after the erev Yom Kippur meal and extending to the following evening. No eating or drinking is permitted.

9. Are there any exceptions?

Yes. Judaism has a deep reverence for life, and, though the Yom Kippur fast is of great importance, it was never allowed to jeopardize health. Those too ill to fast were prohibited from doing so, in spite of their protestations. Those who needed to take medication were allowed to break the fast, as were pregnant women or women who had just given birth. Jews ate in times of famine and plague, as did prisoners in the concentration camps of Nazi Germany. The ancient affirmation of life is just as central in modern times.

10. Should we do anything special at the erev Yom Kippur meal in our home?

Actually, there are some things that should be done before the meal. For example, it is a basic Jewish teaching that Yom Kippur does not atone for wrongs committed against other people, but only for transgressions against God. It therefore has become customary for Jews to seek out friends and relatives whom they have wronged during the year and to personally ask for their forgiveness before Yom Kippur begins. The person asked for forgiveness *must* forgive, and thus Yom Kippur serves a healing function in the community. Yom Kippur is a time when all families should be at peace. Life is too short to indulge in petty arguments or to harbor grudges. Yom Kippur gives

us a yearly opportunity to put aside past hurts and to make a new beginning.

A second set of customs relating to Yom Kippur involves perpetuating the memory of loved ones. Many Jews visit the cemetery the day before Yom Kippur and kindle twenty-four-hour *yahrzeit* candles in memory of departed loved ones. During the Middle Ages, this custom was seen as a means of atonement for the dead. Today, however, it is a beautiful expression of tribute and remembrance.

For the erev Yom Kippur meal, many families have a special *chalah* in the shape of a bird with wings, symbolizing the aspiration of the Jew to ascend spiritually to the level of the angels. When the meal is completed, the family departs for services—a prayer experience unlike any other in the Jewish year. Upon arriving at the synagogue on erev Yom Kippur, one immediately senses a special and unique atmosphere. It is Kol Nidre night, the holiest time of the Jewish year.

11. What is the meaning of Kol Nidre?

Kol Nidre means "all vows" and is the name given to the special liturgical formulation chanted by Jews only on Yom Kippur.

12. Is Kol Nidre a prayer?

No. In fact, Kol Nidre does not even mention God. It is a legal formula for the annulment of vows which dates back many centuries.

13. What is the history of Kol Nidre?

In order to understand the nature and function of Kol Nidre, we must go back to biblical times. It was then common practice for people to make vows that could not possibly be honored. After the Second Temple was destroyed, this practice continued. The leaders of the community were troubled, for they viewed a person's word as his or her bond. Failing to convince the people of the desirability of avoiding rash promises altogether, the rabbis of the Talmud finally created a formal ritual for annulling unkept vows. The original talmudic ceremony took place on the day before Rosh Hashanah. A *bet din* (court) of three judges heard each case. Individuals would come before the court and recite a formula which cancelled vows they had made to themselves or to God. Vows made to other people could only be set aside in the presence of those people and with their consent. This was the practice that laid the groundwork for Kol Nidre.

14. When did Kol Nidre as we know it emerge?

No one knows for certain, but it probably began about the ninth century C.E. Rav Amram's *siddur* (870 C.E.) contains the first complete known text of Kol Nidre, quite different from the talmudic legal formula. Kol Nidre was a collective rather than an individual annulment. A mixture of Hebrew and the then vernacular Aramaic, it cancelled all unintended vows made during the previous year. No one knows who the author was, nor is it clear how the formula came to be associated with Yom Kippur. Nevertheless, despite fierce opposition by the rabbis of many eras, Kol Nidre became a powerful component of the Yom Kippur liturgy.

15. Why would anyone oppose Kol Nidre?

Many leaders of the Jewish community opposed Kol Nidre on the grounds that it offered an easy means of avoiding personal obligation. After all, Kol Nidre made it possible for someone to take a vow, knowing that it could be annulled the following Yom Kippur. (Consider the implications of such a practice for modern legal transactions.) Accordingly, the rabbis narrowed the scope of vows which Kol Nidre could annul. It could not be applied, for example, to promises made to another person. In addition, a twelfth-century change in wording precluded retroactive annulment of vows and focused Kol Nidre only on unmade vows for the future year.

Unfortunately, Kol Nidre also served as a pretext for anti-Semitic slander. During the Middle Ages in particular, Christians used the formula as an excuse for isolating Jews from participation in business, claiming that the word of a Jew could not be trusted.

When the Reform Movement began in nineteenth-century Germany, Kol Nidre was deleted from the liturgy. It was not until 1962 that the text appeared in the *Union Prayer Book* and now in the *Gates of Repentance*. The spiritual power of Kol Nidre among the people resisted every challenge put to it over a period of ten centuries, and it comes down to us today as one of the most beloved liturgical elements in all of Judaism.

16. Who wrote the melody for Kol Nidre?

There have been many different melodies for Kol Nidre. According to a popular myth, the melody we use today was composed by a Spanish Marrano. Other scholars have hypothesized that the melody arose in sixteenth-century Germany. But no one knows for certain, and the music's origin remains mysterious.

The Kol Nidre is chanted three times in traditional synagogues, once in most Reform congregations. The threefold repetition most likely derives from the ancient practice of reciting all official proclamations three times. A beautiful midrash, however, explains this practice in a different way. The first time, says the midrash, Kol Nidre is chanted in a quiet, awe-filled voice, like a servant entering a king's chamber for the first time. The second repetition is a bit louder, symbolic of the servant approaching the royal throne. The third time, the Kol Nidre is sung in full voice, as a subject in the presence of the king, confident of the ruler's mercy and forgiveness.

17. Why do rabbis wear white on Yom Kippur?

Rabbis and many traditional Jews wear white on Yom Kippur. White is a symbol of purity, and, since Yom Kippur is a day when we cleanse ourselves of sin, the color is appropriate. Some also interpret the wearing of white as representing the white garments in which Orthodox Jews are buried. White, then, is seen as a symbol of mortality and as a reminder of the need for humility and repentance.

18. Why do we read the Book of Jonah on Yom Kippur?

The sections of scripture read on each holiday reflect its theme. As Yom Kippur is the Day of Atonement, it is fitting that we read the story of an entire society (the people of Nineveh) that is spared from destruction as a result of true repentance. It is also significant that the citizens of Nineveh are not Jewish. We thus learn that God's mercy and compassion extend to all peoples.

19. Why does Yom Kippur end with a single blast of the shofar?

The stirring sound of the shofar as Yom Kippur ends has many different explanations. Some say that the practice recalls the giving of the Torah at Sinai (when the shofar was blown). Others say that the shofar signals the triumph of Israel over its sins for another year and heralds the possible coming of the Messiah. Finally, there is the superstitious belief that the shofar confuses Satan at a time when he might be tempted to harm the Jewish people.

20. Did you know?

a. The numerical equivalent of the Hebrew *hasatan* (Satan) is 364. A midrash interprets this as indicating that Satan can harm the Jewish people every day of the year, except on Yom Kippur.

b. A common greeting on Yom Kippur is *Gemar Chatimah Tovah*, "May you finally be sealed for good." According to legend, the books of life and death for the coming year were sealed at the close of Yom Kippur. Jews therefore began the custom of wishing one another a kindly fate.

c. There is more than one Yom Kippur. In the sixteenth century, the custom arose of observing a Yom Kippur *katan* (little Yom Kippur) the day before each new moon. Many people fasted, and many of the Yom Kippur confessional prayers were recited every month. Some Jews continue to follow this practice today.

d. The Hebrew word for repentance, *teshuvah*, means "return." In Judaism, repentance is more than pious words. It involves an active turning away from past errors and an active "return" to a just and decent life.

·8·

TU BISHVAT

1. What is Tu Bishvat?

Tu Bishvat, also called Chamishah-Asar Bishvat or the "New Year of the Trees," is Jewish Arbor Day.

2. When do we celebrate Tu Bishvat?

The holiday is observed on the fifteenth day of the Hebrew month of Shevat, roughly corresponding to February in the secular calendar.

3. What does Tu Bishvat mean?

Every letter in Hebrew has a numerical equivalent. Thus, *alef* equals one, *bet* equals two, *gimel* equals three, and so on. The Hebrew letters *tet* (nine) and *vav* (six), used to make up the "Tu" in Tu Bishvat, have a combined numerical value of fifteen (*chamishah-asar* in Hebrew). Tu Bishvat, then, is an abbreviated way of saying Chamishah-Asar Bishvat or "15th of Shevat."

4. Is Tu Bishvat mentioned in the Torah?

No. We first hear of the holiday in the Mishnah, which calls it the "New Year of the Trees," Rosh Hashanah La'ilanot. Scholars believe that Tu Bishvat was originally an agricultural festival, marking the emergence of spring in ancient Palestine. At this time, the tithes on the fruit crop were levied and sent to the Temple in Jerusalem. Some scholars hold that this was also a day for planting trees, especially "marriage trees."

5. What were marriage trees?

It was customary for parents who had been blessed with children during the preceding year to plant special seedlings on the fifteenth of Shevat. Cedars were planted for boys, cypress trees for girls. When the children grew up and married, the trees were cut down and used as part of the *chupah* (marriage canopy). Some Israelis perpetuate this custom today.

6. If Tu Bishvat was a new year, why wasn't it celebrated on the first day of the month? Why the fifteenth?

This question was the subject of spirited debate between the schools of Shammai and Hillel. As we have noted, the two schools argued many fine points of Jewish observance, with the school of Hillel almost always prevailing. In this instance, the school of Shammai advocated the first of Shevat but the school of Hillel proposed the fifteenth as a more practical date, as the climatic conditions would be more favorable. As usual, the position of the school of Hillel was adopted.

7. How was Tu Bishvat transformed from an agricultural festival into the holiday we celebrate today?

As in the case with many Jewish observances, a critical historical event served as a catalyst. After the destruction of the Second Temple (70 C.E.)

and the exile that followed, many Jews felt a need to symbolically bind themselves to their former homeland. Tu Bishvat served in part to fill that spiritual need. As it was no longer possible to bring tithes to the Temple, Jews used this time each year to eat a variety of fruits and nuts that could be obtained from Palestine. The practice, a sort of physical association with the land, continued for many centuries.

The sixteenth and seventeenth-century Kabbalists (mystics) of Palestine elaborated on the exilic customs, creating a ritual for Tu Bishvat somewhat similar to the Passover seder. On erev Tu Bishvat, they would gather in their homes for a fifteen-course meal, each course being one of the foods associated with the land. Between courses they would read from an anthology called *Peri Etz Hadar* (citrus fruit), a compilation of passages on trees drawn from the Bible, the Talmud, and the mystical Zohar. It is interesting to note that the editor of this book was the famous Rabbi Nathan of Gaza. This was the same man who proclaimed Shabbetai Zevi to be the Messiah, a claim that raised Jewish hopes of salvation and then, when shattered, plunged the Jewish community into despair.

Today, in modern Israel, Tu Bishvat has become a national holiday, a tree-planting festival for both Israelis and Jews throughout the world. Much of the credit for the great joy and spirit of the holiday is a direct result of the important work of the Jewish National Fund.

8. What is the Jewish National Fund?

When most of us think of the Jewish National Fund (JNF), we think of the little "blue box" in our homes or the beautiful tree certificates we send or receive at important Jewish moments in our lives and in the lives of family and friends. All too few, however, are fully aware of what JNF has done over the course of many decades to insure the viability of the modern State of Israel. The JNF was the brainchild of a German mathematician named Hermann Schapira. Schapira, an ardent Zionist, realized that there had to be an agency that would purchase the land on which a Jewish state might ultimately flower. He felt that Jews throughout the world should help to buy the land, thus enabling it to be held in trust for the entire Jewish people. The land, he affirmed, must never be sold or mortgaged, only leased. The agency he proposed would ensure that the Jewish state, once established, would never be subject to the whims of real estate speculators or political bodies, whatever their wealth or nationality.

Schapira's brilliant concept was first proposed in 1884. Seventeen years later, in 1901, the Keren Kayemet LeYisrael (JNF) was officially established as the land-purchasing agency of the World Zionist Organization. Since then, JNF has secured countless acres of land; helped to establish *kibbutzim* and *moshavim*; provided those settlements with farm equipment, live stock, and water supply systems; drained swamps; assisted farmers in maximizing crop production; paved thousands of miles of road; built dams for irrigation; and planted over two hundred million trees. Today, Jews in some forty countries help JNF through personal contributions and the purchase of trees. Hospitals, schools, and synagogues are constantly being built on JNF land.

9. How can we plant trees on Tu Bishvat this year?

Almost every congregation has a tree-planting program for families. Children in the religious

school plant trees in honor of, or in memory of, a loved one or friend. Some children plant trees in honor of their parents, brothers and sisters, pets, great Jewish leaders, or even themselves. The Union of American Hebrew Congregations also sponsors special forests in Israel for the entire Reform Movement.

10. Isn't it strange for Judaism to have a special holiday honoring trees?

No, not at all. Trees are part of the natural wonder of our world and have always been a special symbol for Jews. Trees were protected in times of war (Deuteronomy 20:19). A midrashic sage said: "Trees were created for man's companionship." And Rabbi Nachman of Bratzlav proclaimed: "If a man kills a tree before its time, it is as though he had murdered a soul."

Above all, the Torah itself is seen as a "tree of life," a growing and abundant source of spiritual sustenance to a great people. Perhaps this is the best indication of the reverence and respect which Judaism holds for God's world. The tree has been a symbol of life and continues to be a source of life for Israel today. On Tu Bishvat, we celebrate that life in joy and gladness.

·9·

LAG BA'OMER

1. What does Lag Ba'omer mean?

We have seen that every Hebrew letter has a numerical equivalent. The "Tu" in Tu Bishvat, for example, stands for fifteen, hence "15th of Shevat." Likewise, "Lag" consists of two Hebrew letters, *lamed* (thirty) and *gimel* (three). Lag Ba'omer, then, is a shorthand way of saying "the thirty-third day of the *omer*."

2. What is the omer?

The *omer* was an ancient Hebrew measure of grain, amounting to about 3.6 litres. Biblical law (Leviticus 23:9–11) forbade any use of the new barley crop until an *omer* was brought as an offering to the Temple in Jerusalem.

The Book of Leviticus (23:15–16) also commanded: "And from the day on which you bring the offering . . . you shall count off seven weeks. They must be complete." This commandment led to the traditional practice of Sefirat Ha'omer, or "Counting the Omer."

3. Why would biblical law command the counting of seven weeks? Is there anything special about that forty-nine-day period?

Yes. The seven weeks of counting the *omer* spans the forty-nine days between the second day of Pesach and the beginning of Shavuot. Thus, Sefirat Ha'omer links the Exodus from Egypt with the giving of the Torah at Sinai. Jewish mystics expanded upon this historical bond, seeing the period as joining the Jewish people's physical (Pesach) and spiritual (Shavuot) redemption.

After the Temple in Jerusalem was destroyed in 70 C.E., the *omer* offering could no longer be observed. But the practice of counting the *omer* continued and is still observed by many Jews.

4. How do you count the omer?

While few Reform Jews observe this custom, there is a prescribed ritual for counting the *omer*. Each evening of the forty-nine-day period, traditional Jews say a special blessing, recite a prescribed formula for counting each day, then read a psalm and a special prayer. Interestingly, excluding the first verse, the psalm has precisely forty-nine words.

5. That still doesn't explain how the thirty-third day of the omer came to be a Jewish holiday.

Time and time again, Judaism transformed agricultural festivals into commemorations of great historical events. Lag Ba'omer is a perfect example.

The counting of the *omer* was already established as an agricultural and historical experience by the first centuries C.E. But, during that period, a human tragedy invested those weeks with even greater significance. The talmudic scholar Rabbi Akiba (50–137 C.E.) had a school in which thousands of pupils studied. For some unknown reason, a plague descended upon the students, precisely at the time that Sefirat Ha'omer began. For more than four weeks the plague persisted, and more than ten thousand of Akiba's disciples died. Then, miraculously, the plague ended—on the thirty-third day of the *omer*.

Accordingly, the Jews chose both to memorialize the students' deaths and to celebrate the saving of the community from further suffering. Sefirat Ha'omer, therefore, became a period of mourning, except for one day—Lag Ba'omer.

6. Can you tell us more about Rabbi Akiba?

The life of Rabbi Akiba has often served as an inspiration to those who feel that they are "too old" to enhance their knowledge of Judaism. Until the age of forty, Akiba was an ignorant shepherd. At that point in his life, he met a woman named Rachel, daughter of the wealthy Jerusalemite Kalba Savua. It was love at first sight. The couple married secretly, over Kalba Savua's objections, and in spite of his disinheriting his daughter.

Rachel had one goal in life: to enable her husband to pursue the life of scholarship he had always desired. She sent him away to a great academy and worked to support his studies, living alone for many years until he returned. Akiba did come home, with many thousands of students following him and hanging on his every word. When Rachel rushed out to greet her husband, the disciples tried to shunt her aside. But, according to legend, Akiba embraced her and informed his pupils: "Pay this woman the greatest honor, for your wisdom—and mine—are a result of her devotion."

Rabbi Akiba laid the foundation for the editing of the Mishnah, arranging many sections before the great Judah Ha-Nasi took over the awesome task. He might have spent the rest of his life immersed in study had it not been for the Jewish General Bar Kochba.

At that time, Jews lived under Roman rule. Conditions became so oppressive that the people were moved to revolution. Leading the revolt was a man named Bar Kochba ("Son of a Star") whom Akiba believed was the Messiah. He therefore joined the rebellion, which ultimately ended in

defeat and with Bar Kochba's death.

As a retaliatory measure, the Emperor Hadrian prohibited the teaching of Jewish law. Akiba defied the ban and was executed most cruelly, becoming one of ten Jewish martyrs. According to legend, he died with the words of the Shema on his lips, affirming to the last his faith in and commitment to God and the Jewish people.

7. When does Lag Ba'omer fall in the secular calendar?

Lag Ba'omer corresponds to the eighteenth of Iyar in the Hebrew calendar and falls in either May or June of the secular year.

8. What sort of mourning precedes Lag Ba'omer?

Traditional Jews refrain from cutting their hair and attending dinners where music is played. It is also traditionally a time when no Jewish weddings are permitted. The mourning is set aside on Lag Ba'omer, making it a day of special joy and festivity. The ban on festive occasions has now been lifted so that Jews can celebrate the fifth of Iyar, Yom Ha'atzmaut, Israel Independence Day.

9. How do we celebrate Lag Ba'omer?

Lag Ba'omer is not mentioned in the Torah and only hinted at in the Talmud. Consequently, there is no formal ritual, but rather a series of customs which the people found attractive and meaningful.

Many weddings take place on Lag Ba'omer. In the Israeli community of Meron, it has become a day when three-year-old children get their first haircuts. Parties and picnics abound, and, at least in Israel, hundreds of people attend midnight bonfires and many children carry little bows and arrows.

10. Why midnight bonfires?

The Jewish historian Josephus recorded Lag Ba'omer as the date in 66 C.E. when the revolt against Rome began. There was a great victory on that day. It is therefore likely that the bonfires of today commemorate the bonfires kindled almost 2,000 years ago in celebration of successful Jewish resistance to oppression.

11. What about the bows and arrows?

Scholars offer two explanations. The first relates to Bar Kochba's victory. Since soldiers used bows and arrows as their primary weapons, we carry them on Lag Ba'omer to remember their courage.

Second, in addition to its other historical associations, Lag Ba'omer was the day on which the great Simeon Bar Yochai died. Bar Yochai, a bril-

liant mystic and traditionally cited as the author of the mystical Zohar, is said to have been so righteous that no rainbows appeared in the world during his lifetime. According to the Torah, the first rainbow was God's assurance to Noah that He would never again destroy the world by flood. Legend has it that no such assurances were even necessary while Simeon Bar Yochai was alive, so great was his goodness and positive influence on others. Each year on Lag Ba'omer, Jews from all over the world come to Meron to visit Bar Yochai's grave, a moving tribute to a great figure in Jewish history.

12. Lag Ba'omer sounds similar to May Day. Are there any parallels?

Yes. Some say that at least a few of the Lag Ba'omer customs were borrowed from May Day as celebrated in western Europe during the Middle Ages. Then it was customary to take long walks in the woods, light bonfires, and shoot arrows at "evil spirits." Advocates of this "borrowing" theory hold that the customs were then invested with particularly Jewish interpretations.

Lag Ba'omer, then, is a day rich in historical and spiritual significance. But no day was more important in Jewish history than the day the Jewish people received the Torah. Just two weeks after Lag Ba'omer we celebrate Shavuot, the festival of the Giving of the Law.

·10·
SHAVUOT

1. What is the meaning of Shavuot?

Shavuot is a Hebrew word meaning "weeks" and refers to the Jewish festival marking the giving of the Torah at Mount Sinai.

2. When do we celebrate Shavuot?

Shavuot falls on the sixth and seventh days of the Hebrew month of Sivan, corresponding to May or June of the secular calendar. Orthodox and Conservative Jews celebrate two days of the holiday, while most Reform Jews observe one day.

3. How did Shavuot originate?

Shavuot, like so many other Jewish holidays, began as an ancient agricultural festival. In biblical times, it marked the end of the spring barley harvest and the beginning of the summer wheat harvest. As with the other two Jewish "pilgrimage festivals," Pesach and Sukot, Shavuot was distinguished by the bringing of crop offerings to the Temple in Jerusalem. Reflecting the original nature of the festival, the Torah refers to it as Chag Hakatzir (Festival of the Harvest), Yom Habikurim (Day of the First Fruits), and Chag Hashavuot (Festival of Weeks).

After the Temple in Jerusalem was destroyed and offerings were no longer possible, Jews began to decorate their homes and synagogues with greenery and flowers, a custom preserved in numerous Jewish households today. In addition, many citizens of the modern State of Israel maintain the spirit of the ancient sacrifice by selling the first fruits of their harvest and donating the proceeds to the Jewish National Fund.

4. When did Shavuot become the Festival of the Giving of Torah?

The interpretation of Shavuot as the Festival of the Giving of Torah is most significant to us as modern Jews. It dates from biblical times and helps to explain the holiday's most common name, "Weeks." We have already studied the custom of counting the *omer*, the practice of numbering the forty-nine days (seven weeks) beginning with the second day of Pesach. The Torah tells us that it took precisely that amount of time for our ancestors to travel from Egypt to the foot of Mount Sinai. Thus, Leviticus 23:21 commands: "And you shall proclaim that day (the fiftieth day) to be a holy convocation. . . ." Hellenistic Jews of the third century B.C.E. called the holiday Pentecost, from two Greek words meaning "fifty." The name Shavuot, then, symbolizes the completion of a seven-week journey, a pilgrimage that led from a life of oppression to the giving of the Torah. It is the only major festival with no Torah-prescribed calendar date. We count the weeks and then rejoice.

5. When did Shavuot, as we know it today, begin to emerge?

Shavuot began sometime after the destruction

of the Second Temple. The Mishnah refers to Shavuot as *Zeman Matan Toratenu*, the "Time of the Giving of the Law." By that period, it was already customary on Shavuot to read the section of the Torah containing the Ten Commandments and the Book of Ruth.

6. Why do we read the Book of Ruth on Shavuot?

Ruth, one of the five "scrolls" or *megillot* read on special holidays during the Jewish year, is particularly appropriate for Shavuot.

After a series of painful family tragedies, the story relates, Ruth journeyed with her mother-in-law Naomi and her sister-in-law Orpah on the road back to Naomi's homeland in Judah. Realizing that Ruth and Orpah would have difficulty in adjusting to life in Judah, Naomi urged them to remain in Moab, their birthplace. Orpah turned back, but Ruth refused: "Entreat me not to leave thee and to return from following after thee; for whither thou goest, I will go; and where thou lodgest, I will lodge; thy people shall be my people and thy God my God" (1:16–17).

(Later commentators note that this speech was not only an expression of loyalty and devotion but also a formal act of conversion to Judaism. Surprisingly, Ruth was not Jewish.)

Ruth continued with Naomi, settling with her and caring for her, going out to the fields each day to gather that part of the harvest left for the poor in accordance with Jewish law. The owner of the field, Boaz, a distant relative of Naomi, fell in love with Ruth and married her. Their child, Obed, became the father of Jesse, the father of David. Thus, the loyal convert Ruth was the great-grandmother of David, King of Israel.

Three reasons are offered as explanations for reading Ruth on Shavuot. First, and most obviously, the story takes place during the summer harvest. Second, the Book reminds us of our responsibility to Judaism. If Ruth, a convert, could be so committed to Judaism in spite of many obstacles, we too can find a continual source of blessing in our tradition. Finally, say some scholars, we read the Book of Ruth because it reminds us of the great King David.

7. What does King David have to do with Shavuot?

Jewish folklore holds that Shavuot marks both the day of birth and death of King David. (Abraham's death was also thought to have occurred on the festival, as was the birth of the patriarch Isaac.) To this day, Jews read Psalms (traditionally ascribed to David) on Shavuot. In Israel, hundreds of Jews make Shavuot pilgrimages to Mount Zion and King David's tomb. In a few traditional synagogues throughout the world, 150 candles are lit, one for each of the 150 psalms, in memory of this great Jewish leader.

8. Are there any other special customs associated with Shavuot?

Yes. Continuing a practice begun by mystics of the sixteenth century, many Jews stay up all night on Shavuot. They read from a special volume containing sections from the beginning and end of every book in the Bible and the Mishnah. This custom, Tikun Leil Shavuot, symbolizes commitment to Torah. But it also sets us apart from our wilderness ancestors. According to legend, the night before the Torah was given at Sinai, the Jews in the desert all fell asleep, and Moses had to wake them up to receive their precious inheritance. Not so with us. We are always ready to receive the Torah.

Traditional Jewish families have two *chalot* on Shavuot, one for each of the tablets of law. It is also customary to eat dairy dishes on the holiday, especially cheesecake and blintzes. This delicious practice symbolizes the sweetness of Torah, the "land of milk and honey" which the Jews were about to enter, and the necessity of avoiding idolatrous incidents such as that of the golden calf (symbolized by meat). Also, the ceremony of Confirmation is related to Shavuot.

9. How did Confirmation begin?

First instituted in Germany in 1810, and introduced into North America at New York's Congregation Emanu-El in 1847, the Confirmation service quickly became a popular and universal Reform rite for boys and girls, in place of *bar mitzvah* for boys only. In fact, many Conservative congregations gradually adopted Confirmation as well.

Slowly, the powerful attraction of *bar mitzvah* reasserted itself in Reform congregations. *Bat mitzvah* was added for girls. But Confirmation remained, a uniquely Reform creation which invested Shavuot with contemporary significance.

10. Why hold Confirmation on Shavuot?

Just as our ancestors stood at Sinai to receive the Torah, so is Confirmation a time when Jews prepare to confirm their membership in the Jewish people. Some Jews confirm that commitment in ninth or tenth grade, others in adult Confirmation ceremonies. But Confirmation, whenever it occurs, captures an important message of Shavuot.

The Jews who came out of Egypt were not truly free until they accepted the responsibility of Torah, the necessity for self-discipline and lives filled with Jewish values. They were not totally liberated until, as a people, they said: *Naaseh venishma*, "We will do and we will hear." It is no accident, I believe, that Shavuot is called *Zeman Matan Toratenu*, the "Time of the Giving of the Law"— giving, not receiving. The Torah is ours for the taking. But only we, through our actions, can receive it and make it our personal possession, all the days of our lives.

·11·

TISHAH BE'AV

1. What is the meaning of Tishah Be'av?

Tishah Be'av means "Ninth of Av" and refers to a traditional Jewish day of fasting and mourning. Av corresponds to July or August of the secular year.

2. What does Tishah Be'av commemorate?

For traditional Jews, Tishah Be'av is the darkest of all days, a time set aside for mourning the destruction of both ancient Temples in Jerusalem.

3. Why was the Temple in Jerusalem so important?

In contrast to Orthodoxy, Reform Judaism has never assigned a central religious role to the ancient Temple. To understand the mournful nature of Tishah Be'av, then, we must enter the traditional mind as we look back into history.

The First Temple in Jerusalem was constructed during the reign of King Solomon (965 B.C.E–925 B.C.E). Solomon's father, King David, had wished to build the Temple, but was not allowed to do so. The Bible relates that God disqualified David because of his many military campaigns. The Temple was to be a holy place, a place of peace. Therefore, only a king who had not shed blood could bring it into being. Thus, Solomon, whose Hebrew name was Shlomo (from shalom, peace), inherited this sacred task.

Solomon built the First Temple with the assis-

tance of King Hiram of Tyre. Hiram sent his Phoenician artists and builders magnificent stone from his nation's quarries and the beautiful cedars of Lebanon to aid in the task. The Bible tells us that no iron tools were used in the work, as iron was a material of weapons and war. In an attempt to explain how work proceeded without these iron implements, a legend arose of a shamir worm that had the capacity to split rocks!

The finished Temple was an awesome structure. Situated on a mountain 2,500 feet high, it had courtyards, a sanctuary, and a small room called the Holy of Holies, entered only once a year by the high priest. It was in the Temple that the kohanim (high priests) offered the ancient sacrifices on behalf of the people, assisted by the Levites.

4. Is that where we got the three categories of Jews?

Yes. At one time every Jew fell into one of three categories: kohen, Levite, or Israelite. A kohen was a priest, a Levite a Temple assistant, and an Israelite one of the "masses." One's status was passed on through one's father. Today, these categories are not as important as they once were. Among traditional Jews, there is still some recognition of differential status, especially during the weekly reading of the Torah and during special Yom Kippur, festival, and life cycle rituals.

Certain names hint at the status our families

might once have occupied, especially: Cohen, Kahan, Katz (*kohen*), and Levy (Levite). But most of us can safely assume that we are descended from Israelites.

5. What happened to the First Temple?

In 586 B.C.E., the Babylonian army surrounded Jerusalem. Led by their general, Nebuchadnezzar, they broke into the city and conquered it. Then, on the Ninth of Av, they destroyed the Temple. The Jews were sent into exile, crushed and despondent. According to some scholars, the prophet Jeremiah, grieving for the Temple, composed Psalm 137, in which he wrote: "By the waters of Babylon, we lay down and wept for thee Zion." A people who had grounded their entire religious system in a priestly Temple structure suddenly had it torn away from them.

6. What happened then?

Even as he mourned, Jeremiah still had hope. He told the people that they would one day return to Jerusalem and rebuild the Temple. He was correct. Some sixty years later, Persia conquered Babylonia, and the Persian King Cyrus allowed the Jews to return home. They rebuilt the Temple, but it was not nearly as magnificent as Solomon's Temple had been. Still, the Jews rejoiced, for once again they had an opportunity to be led by their priests and to offer sacrifices in their holiest site.

It was this rebuilt Temple that King Antiochus defiled in 168 B.C.E., and which the Maccabees reconsecrated three years later. But the building of the Second Temple was yet to come.

7. Who expanded the Second Temple?

The Second Temple was enhanced and expanded during the first century B.C.E. by King Herod, one of the cruelest rulers in Jewish history. Herod was a tyrant, a paranoid personality, with an ego of enormous proportion. The ancient Israeli fortress at Masada was created by Herod in order to protect him from any enemy, real or imagined. (Modern visitors to Masada, who now ascend by cable car, often gasp in amazement at the seemingly impenetrable fortifications. As we know, however, Masada was eventually conquered.)

Deciding that the rebuilt Temple was not to his liking, Herod decided to expand it. He partially leveled the previous site, then oversaw the construction of a Temple that rivaled that of Solomon in grandeur.

8. What happened to the Second Temple?

Herod had intended to continually add new structures to the Temple grounds, but the work was never completed. In 70 C.E., Roman legions, led by the General Titus, conquered Jerusalem and destroyed the Temple. It was the Ninth of Av. Once again, the Jews were sent into exile, this time to Rome. There, in shame, many were led through the Arch of Titus, built to honor the great conqueror. To this day, most Jews will not walk through the arch, and many will spit on it as they pass by.

9. So that's why Tishah Be'av became so important?

Yes. Some historians have expressed doubt that the actual destruction of both Temples occurred on the Ninth of Av, but there is no disputing the fact that the day became a symbol of Jewish tragedy. The synagogue ultimately replaced the Temple. The three daily worship services were substituted for the Temple's three daily sacrifices.

The rabbi filled the leadership role once held by the *kohen.* But Jews never lost hope that the Temple would be restored. Their prayer books and their songs expressed their yearning, and Tishah Be'av became a vehicle for expressing their deep sorrow. Over the centuries, other great tragedies were linked to Tishah Be'av. Some of the Crusades' most brutal massacres were said to have occurred on this day. The expulsion edict from Spain was supposedly issued on the Ninth of Av in 1492. And, of course, many Jews remember victims of Nazi genocide on Tishah Be'av.

10. What religious practices are associated with Tishah Be'av?

Tishah Be'av is marked by a twenty-four-hour fast, as well as by certain customs common to *shivah,* the period of mourning following a family death.

Many traditional Jews begin a period of semi-mourning three weeks before Tishah Be'av on the seventeenth of Tamuz. It was supposedly on this day in 586 B.C.E. that the Babylonians first breached Jerusalem's walls. Beginning on this date and through the Ninth of Av, pious Jews have no weddings, haircuts, or festive celebrations.

The mourning intensifies on the first of Av. No meat or wine is consumed. No new clothing is purchased and shaving is forbidden. On the evening before Tishah Be'av, a total fast begins. As on Yom Kippur, the fast extends until the following sundown. In the synagogue, the Book of Lamentations is chanted, as are *kinot,* dirges written during the Middle Ages. Sitting on low stools, a *shivah* custom, congregants also read sections of the books of Jeremiah and Job, as well as biblical and talmudic passages dealing with the Temples' destruction.

Interestingly, Jews do not study Torah except for those passages already mentioned. This is because Torah study is joyful and thus not permitted during Tishah Be'av. In most Sephardic synagogues, the ark is draped in black, with only the *ner tamid* (eternal light) and candles illuminating the sanctuary.

11. Why don't most Reform Jews observe Tishah Be'av?

To the early Reformers, mourning the destruction of the Temple in such elaborate fashion did not seem meaningful, especially since Reform did not idealize the rebuilding of the Temple as Orthodoxy had done. To Reform, then, 586 B.C.E. and 70 C.E. are important dates in Jewish history, but Tishah Be'av has faded in importance as a ritual observance.

12. Don't the modern State of Israel and the reunification of Jerusalem technically signify a rebuilding of the Temple?

Many Jews believe so, and many Israelis do not observe Tishah Be'av for just this reason. But some pious Jews still await the rebuilding of the ancient Temple, the restoration of the priestly system, and their opportunity to once again fulfill all the *mitzvot* delineated in the Torah.

One thing is certain. The Western Wall, the imposing surrounding wall of Solomon's Temple, is now in Jewish hands. The tiny scraps of paper placed between its ancient stones carry the prayers of Jews from all over the world. What stories the wall could tell—stories of Jewish tragedy and triumph. And I, for one, would like to believe that it would say to us that we Jews have kept the Temple alive—wherever we have been—by creating a Judaism that flourished and thrived.

·12·
SUKOT

Some Historical Background

1. What is the meaning of Sukot?

Sukot, a Hebrew word meaning "booths" or "huts," refers to the annual Jewish festival giving thanks for a bountiful fall harvest and commemorating the forty years of Jewish wandering in the desert after Sinai.

2. When do we celebrate Sukot?

Sukot begins five days after Yom Kippur, on the fifteenth day of the Hebrew month of Tishrei. The holiday, which falls in either September or October of the secular calendar, is observed for seven days by Israeli and Reform Jews and for eight days by traditional Jews living outside of Israel.

3. Does Sukot have any other names?

Yes. The Bible refers to the festival as Chag Hasukot, the Feast of Booths (Leviticus 23:34), Chag Haasif, the Feast of Ingathering (Exodus 23:16), and simply Hechag, *The* Festival (I Kings 8:2). In addition, as the liturgy of rabbinic times emerged centuries later, the holiday was also designated Zeman Simchatenu, the Season of Our Joy.

4. How did Sukot originate?

Like many societies, the ancient Hebrews had a variety of agricultural festivals. Sukot probably began as one of these ceremonial expressions of thanks to God for a good crop. By biblical times, Sukot had developed into the celebration of the

summer fruit harvest: "At the end of the year, when you gather in your produce from the fields" (Exodus 23:16).

Sukot became one of the three Jewish pilgrimage festivals (Shalosh Regalim). As on Pesach and Shavuot, the people would bring a portion of their harvest's first fruits to the Temple in Jerusalem. There it would be offered as a sacrifice to God by the High Priest (kohen).

The holiday that became Sukot initially had no fixed date and was observed whenever the harvest had been completed, depending on climatic conditions. By Torah times, however, the Book of Leviticus (23:34) declared: "On the fifteenth day of the seventh month, there shall be a Feast of Tabernacles to the Lord for seven days." The date, then, was standardized. And, as was the case with so many agricultural celebrations, the holiday was invested with strong historical signifi-

cance. Just as Pesach had been tied to the Exodus, and Shavuot associated with the giving of the Torah, Sukot came to reflect the wilderness experience. The forty years of wandering in the desert prior to entering the Promised Land was captured, symbolically, in the frail sukah: "For in booths did I make the Children of Israel dwell when I brought them out of the land of Egypt" (Leviticus 23:43).

5. What happened to Sukot after the destruction of the Temple?

After 70 C.E., when temple sacrifices were no longer possible, Sukot underwent the same sort of metamorphosis that enabled other Jewish festivals to survive and retain their religious power. Sukot became a synagogue and home celebration, marked by unique rituals and symbols.

The Sukah

1. What is the meaning of sukah?

Sukah is a Hebrew word meaning "hut" or "booth" and refers to the special structure erected by Jews during the festival of Sukot. Sukah is a singular noun, Sukot the plural of the same word.

2. What does the sukah symbolize?

The sukah symbolizes the frail huts in which the Israelites lived during their forty years of wandering in the desert after the Exodus from Egypt. It also serves to remind Jews of the biblical account of how God protected them, provided for their needs in the wilderness, and, by implication, still watches over us today.

3. Where is the sukah first mentioned?

The Book of Leviticus (23:42–43) portrays God as commanding: "You shall dwell in booths for seven days . . . that your generations may know that I made the Children of Israel to dwell in booths, when I brought them out of the land of Egypt."

The sukah, then, dates back to biblical times, an ancient symbol that has retained its power and religious significance for over 2,000 years.

4. How do you build a sukah?

Jewish law is quite explicit in outlining the structural and decorative design of the traditional sukah. It is to have at least three walls with a superstructure, while the fourth may be open. The walls may be constructed of any material, generally canvas, wood, or metal.

The roof is to be temporary, covered with loose branches from trees or anything which grows out of the ground and has been cut off from the ground. According to tradition, this roof covering, sechach, should give shade and yet allow those in the sukah to see the stars through the roof at night. There is no prescribed size for the traditional sukah, so long as it accommodates at least one person.

Once the sukah is built, it is common to decorate it by hanging fruit from the sechach, putting posters on the walls, and even laying carpet on the floor.

5. You make the sukah seem almost like a home.

For traditional Jews and some Reform Jews,

the *sukah* becomes a second home during the holiday. Taking the commandment to "dwell in booths" literally, these Jews eat all their meals and even live in the *sukah* for the duration of the festival.

Most Reform congregants have grown accustomed to the beautiful *sukot* erected in their temples each year. But numerous Jews the world over have *sukot* for their families and derive great pleasure in making their backyard *sukah* a family project. Some congregations even have prizes for the most attractive family *sukah*. You may decide to build your own *sukah* this year. If so, be assured that it will be a lovely and meaningful Jewish experience.

6. Are there any special rituals for the sukah?

Yes. Especially on the first two nights, tradition calls for the family to enter the *sukah,* recite the *Motzi* prayer over the meal to be eaten, and then to add a special blessing: *Baruch Atah Adonai Elohenu Melech ha'olam asher kideshanu bemitzvotav vetzivanu leishev basukah.* "Blessed are You, O Lord our God, Ruler of the world, who has made us holy through *mitzvot* and commanded us to dwell in the *sukah.*"

Another custom of Sukot involves extending hospitality, especially to the needy. Tradition tells us that there are certain guests of the festival, *ushpizin,* who are present in spirit in every *sukah*: Abraham, Isaac, Jacob, Moses, Aaron, David. In addition, many Jews will invite guests outside of their families to join them for a holiday meal.

Hospitality to strangers is a recurrent theme in Jewish literature. One midrash relates that the Jews were protected during their desert wanderings because of Abraham's hospitality to three strangers who came to his tent.

Little wonder then that Sukot, with its ties to the wilderness experience, places such emphasis on graciously receiving and welcoming others into our homes.

There are at least two more symbols associated with Sukot that deserve our careful attention. Rich in significance, replete with special rituals, the *lulav* and the *etrog* are central to this joyous harvest and historical festival.

The Lulav and the Etrog

1. What does lulav mean?

Lulav is a Hebrew word meaning "palm branch" and refers to a unique ceremonial object associated with the holiday of Sukot.

2. What is a lulav?

Lulav is a generic term, describing a three-sectioned holder with a single palm branch in the center, two willow branches on the left, and three myrtle branches on the right.

3. What does etrog mean?

Etrog is a Hebrew word meaning "citron" and refers to the special lemon-like fruit used in conjunction with the *lulav* in the Sukot ritual.

4. How did the lulav and the etrog come to be associated with Sukot?

Sukot originated as a harvest festival, with the crop's first fruits brought to the Temple in Jerusalem as an offering to God. As part of the celebration, the Book of Leviticus 23:40 commands: "On the first day, you shall take the fruit of a goodly tree (etrog), palm branches, myrtle boughs, and willows and rejoice before the Lord."

The use of the *lulav* and *etrog* as ceremonial objects, then, originated in biblical times. Over the centuries, the combination of citron, palm, myrtle, and willow also became known as the *arbaah minim* or four species.

5. How do we perform the ritual of the lulav and etrog?

Traditional Jews perform the ritual of the *lulav* and *etrog* each day during morning prayers.

The traditional ritual proceeds as follows:

a. Facing east, the *lulav* is placed in the right hand and the *etrog* in the left. The spine of the *lulav* faces the holder, with the myrtle on the right and the willows on the left. The hands are then brought together so that the *lulav* and *etrog* are side by side.

b. Next, a special blessing is recited: *Baruch Atah Adonai Elohenu Melech ha'olam asher kideshanu bemitzvotav vetzivanu al netilat lulav.* "Blessed are You, O Lord our God, Ruler of the universe, who has made us holy through *mitzvot* and ordained the taking of the *lulav.*"

c. On the first day of the festival, the *Shehecheyanu* prayer is also added.

d. Finally, the *lulav* is shaken in all directions—east, south, west, north, up, and down—while reciting or chanting *Hodu L'Adonai ki Tov ki le'olam Chasdo.* "Give thanks to the Lord for He is Good, for His loving-kindness endures forever."

A suggested Reform home ceremony for Sukot may be found in the CCAR's *Gates of the House: The New Union Home Prayer Book.*

6. Did the rabbis invest the lulav and etrog with greater symbolic significance over time?

Yes. There are a rich assortment of ancient and modern midrashic interpretations of the *lulav* and *etrog*, all of which teach important Jewish values.

The shaking of the *lulav* in all directions, for example, was seen as an affirmation of God's omnipresence. The *lulav*, according to some, was symbolic of the Hebrew letter "*vav*" in the Hebrew name of God—*yod, hei, vav, hei*—Adonai.

In addition, each of the four species was interpreted as representing different parts of the body, joined together in serving God. The willow was the mouth, uttering prayer; the *etrog* the heart, seat of wisdom and understanding; the *lulav* the spine, symbolic of upright character; and the myrtle the eyes, tools of learning and enlightenment. Then, too, holding the *lulav* and *etrog* together was seen by some as symbolizing the unity of the Jewish people.

Finally, the four species took on the qualities of different types of human beings. With smell equated with righteous deeds and taste likened to learning, the rabbis generated a unique typology. The *etrog*, with both taste and smell, represents the person who is knowledgeable and performs good deeds. The myrtle, with smell but no taste, is the person who is righteous but ignorant. The *lulav* has a taste but no smell, indicative of one who is learned but does not engage in righteous acts. The willow, with neither taste nor smell, is the sort of person we'd all rather avoid.

One is struck by the creativity and imagination of the rabbis, who were able to increase the symbolic power of the simplest objects of nature through their sensitivity and brilliance.

Hoshana Rabbah, Shemini Atzeret, Simchat Torah

As Sukot comes to an end, we encounter three more special days in the Jewish calendar. One, Simchat Torah, is familiar to us. Two others, Hoshana Rabbah and Shemini Atzeret, are not as widely known or observed in Reform congregations. All three, however, have a great deal to teach us about Jewish ideas, values, and outlook.

1. What is the meaning of Hoshana Rabbah?
Hoshana Rabbah, Hebrew for the "Great Hoshana," is a name given to the seventh day of Sukot. Orthodox and Conservative Jews outside of Israel celebrate Sukot for eight days, while Reform and Israeli Jews celebrate for seven days. Thus, this traditional observance is the second-to-last day of Sukot for Orthodox and Conservative congregations.

2. What is Hoshana?
Hoshana is a contraction of the Hebrew phrase *hoshiah na* (Psalms 118:25) which means "we beseech You, O Lord, save us now." During the Sukot festival, the psalm is chanted every day, including the seventh day, when some Jews carry willow twigs called *hoshanot*. The twin meanings are joined in the Hoshana Rabbah ritual.

3. How did Hoshana Rabbah originate?
Sukot was not only a time of thanks for a bountiful harvest. During the days of the Temple, Jews saw it as an additional opportunity for seeking

7. How can we get a lulav and etrog?
Check with your rabbi. Many communities have one or more Jewish book or gift shops that will order a *lulav* and *etrog* for you. If you live in the New York area, you can visit the Lower East Side just before the holiday. There you will see dozens of tables covered with *lulavim* and *etrogim*. It's a real experience shopping carefully and selecting a *lulav* and *etrog* just right for you and your family.

forgiveness for their sins. Though Yom Kippur remained the central day of atonement, throughout Sukot Jews implored God to "save us now." In Temple times, on each of the first six days of Sukot, Jews would have single processions, or *hakafot*, around the altar while chanting the *hoshiah na*. On the seventh day, seven circuits were made (hence the "Great Hoshana") while reciting this special prayer. Afterwards, they would beat willow twigs against the ground at the sides of the altar. The falling leaves were a symbol of sins which they now removed.

4. Why this elaborate ritual?
Jews came to believe that the books of judgment were finally sealed on Hoshana Rabbah. Hence the passionate "last chance" plea for forgiveness.

5. Is Hoshana Rabbah observed today?
Most Reform temples do not mark Hoshana Rabbah, but Orthodox and Conservative congregations preserve the essence of the biblical rite. Seven *hakafot* or processions are made around the synagogue. Worshipers carry the *lulav* and *etrog* while reciting the Hoshana prayer for deliverance. In addition, traditional Jews will beat willow twigs against the synagogue pews until all the leaves have been broken off, a symbol of "breaking off" sins accumulated during the year.

6. Is it only a coincidence that Hoshana Rabbah falls on the seventh day of Sukot and involves seven hakafot around the sanctuary?
We are not sure. Certainly the number seven has many possible interpretations. Some see this ritual as a reenactment of the Jewish people's

seven-circuit march around the walls of Jericho under Joshua's leadership (Joshua 6:12–15). Others hold that the seven *hakafot* symbolize the seven days of creation and thus a potential spiritual rebirth of each person for the year to come. Whatever the reason, however, it is clear that Hoshana Rabbah was and is a deeply religious affirmation of God's saving power and of the individual's accountability for personal actions.

7. What is the meaning of Shemini Atzeret?

Shemini Atzeret is Hebrew for "eighth-day convocation" and is the name given to the eighth day of Sukot.

8. Is Shemini Atzeret biblically based?

Yes. Leviticus 23:36 proclaims: "On the eighth day you shall observe a holy convocation." Jews in biblical times observed Sukot for seven days. For them, this eighth day came after Sukot; for Orthodox and Conservative Jews today, it is the last day of the Sukot festival.

9. What was the purpose of Shemini Atzeret?

Shemini Atzeret was originally a time of reflection on the holy days of Sukot which had just ended. Jews who left their booths engaged in a final day of prayer before returning to their daily routine. Over time, Shemini Atzeret also became a day on which Jews recited a special prayer for rain in the year to come—quite appropriate in view of Sukot's agricultural motif. In addition, some Jews stressed a second meaning of the word *atzeret* in interpreting the holiday. *Atzeret* can denote either "convocation" or a sense of "pausing and waiting." Accordingly, one rabbinic parable spoke of Shemini Atzeret as God's way of prolonging a close relationship with the people of Israel: "God is like a king who invites all his children to a feast lasting a set number of days. But, when the time arrives for them to depart, he says, 'My children, I have a request. Stay one more day. Your leaving is hard for me.'" The solemnity of Shemini Atzeret, then, gives way to the joy and excitement of Simchat Torah.

10. What is the meaning of Simchat Torah?

Simchat Torah is Hebrew for "rejoicing in the Law" and refers to the celebration each year when Jews read the concluding section of the Book of Deuteronomy (the fifth book of the Torah) and start with Genesis once again.

11. Is Simchat Torah as old as Sukot?

No, not as we know it today. Only in the eleventh century did the day (the ninth day after the beginning of Sukot) take on both the name and the festive ritual of what we now recognize as Simchat Torah.

12. Why did Simchat Torah develop so late?

Simchat Torah celebrates the continuing commitment of the Jew to the study of Torah. At this season each year, we complete our annual reading of the Torah and begin the process over again. In doing so, we affirm our view of Torah as a tree of life and demonstrate a living example of never-ending lifelong study.

Obviously, an annual holiday of this nature implies a one-year cycle of Torah reading. But that was not always the case. In ancient Palestine, Jews followed a triennial, or three-year, cycle of Torah reading. The one-year cycle was a custom of the Babylonian Jewish community. It was not until the eighth century that the great majority of Jews adopted the annual system. Indeed, as late as the nineteenth century, some Reform congregations in the United States and Germany still preserved the three-year cycle.

Simchat Torah as an annual observance, then, emerged only after the great debate over the Torah reading cycle had been fairly well resolved.

13. How do we celebrate Simchat Torah?

Simchat Torah is a joyous celebration. The Torah scrolls are taken from the ark and carried by congregants around the synagogue seven times. During these seven circuits, or *hakafot*, those not carrying Torahs will often wave brightly colored flags and sing Hebrew songs. The Torah service is the major event of the Simchat Torah celebration. One member of the congregation opens the Torah and reads the last section of the Book of Deuteronomy. Traditionally, this individual is called the *"chatan Torah,"* or the "bridegroom of Torah." A second person then opens another Torah scroll and reads the opening section of Genesis, *Bereshit* in Hebrew. This person is traditionally referred to as the *"chatan Bereshit"* or "bride-

groom of *Bereshit.*" It is considered a great honor to have a part in this important ritual, and those invited to do so are usually the leaders of the Jewish community.

14. Simchat Torah seems somewhat like a wedding.

Yes. In fact, many scholars interpret the Simchat Torah ritual as a symbolic "wedding" of the Jewish people to Torah. When we study life cycle ceremonies together, we will see the many parallels between the traditional marriage ritual and Simchat Torah, among them the seven circles that the traditional bride makes around the groom and the use of the terms "bridegroom of Torah" and "bridegroom of *Bereshit.*" Since Reform congregations do not limit the reading of Torah to men, however, the traditional terminology has passed out of use in Reform temples.

15. Why do we carry flags on Simchat Torah?

The origin of this custom is unclear. Some scholars hold that the marching with flags recaptures the history of the ancient twelve tribes of Israel, when each tribe had its own banner. Other scholars believe that this practice originated in the Middle Ages as a cultural borrowing from certain Christian customs.

16. Are there any other special customs associated with Simchat Torah?

In most Orthodox and Conservative synagogues, and in some Reform congregations, all children who have not yet reached the age of *bar* or *bat mitzvah* are called to the Torah. Before the entire congregation, with a *talit* spread above their heads, the children receive a special blessing from the rabbi. In Reform temples, Simchat Torah is also a time when children just entering religious school are called to the *bimah* and blessed in the beautiful ceremony of consecration.

The symbolic message of these customs and of Simchat Torah speaks to every Jew in every generation. The Torah is the possession of the Jewish people. It is our heritage, our history, our very life. Its teachings have served as a bond, linking Jews, young and old, over many generations, over time and space, in every land where we have lived. And the words that we utter as we end the reading of the Torah and begin again each year are the powerful words that have inspired us throughout our history: *Chazak, chazak, venitchazek.* "Be strong, be strong, and let us be of good courage," building a living Judaism through study, action, and commitment.

·13·

BERIT MILAH, BERIT HACHAYIM

Berit Milah: Some Historical Background

1. What is the meaning of berit milah?

Berit milah (literally, "covenant of circumcision"), refers to a religious ritual through which male babies are formally welcomed into the Jewish people.

2. What is a circumcision?

Circumcision is a surgical operation in which the foreskin is removed from the penis. While today many male babies are routinely circumcised, Judaism sets the medical procedure in the context of a significant religious ceremony.

3. Did berit milah originate with the Jews?

If one speaks only of the rite of circumcision, Judaism cannot claim credit for its origins. To many ancient peoples, circumcision was a central observance, a rite of puberty or fertility, signaling the attainment of manhood at age twelve or thirteen, but a tribal rather than a religious practice. Today, certain peoples of Africa, Ethiopia, and other countries practice circumcision in this fashion, often as much a test of courage as a formal tribal custom. Judaism, however, took the rite of circumcision and invested it with deep spiritual

and religious significance. *Berit milah* emerged as the symbol of a covenant between God and the Jewish people.

4. How did berit milah begin?

Berit milah is the oldest religious rite in Judaism, dating back almost 4,000 years. It is first mentioned in Genesis 17, when God "says" to Abraham: "Every male among you shall be circumcised. You shall circumcise the flesh of your foreskin, and that shall be the sign of the covenant between Me and you. At the age of eight days, every male among you throughout the generations shall be circumcised, even the homeborn slave. . . . An uncircumcised male . . . has broken My covenant." According to the Torah, Abraham immediately followed God's command, circumcising himself, his son Ishmael, and all the males of his household. Abraham was ninety-nine years old at the time of his circumcision, while Ishmael was thirteen, which may serve in part to explain the common practice among some peoples of circumcision at puberty. From that time forward, however, Jewish males were circumcised at the age of eight days, not as a symbol of fertility, but as a sign of their membership in a covenant people.

5. Did Judaism evolve any substitute for the pagan rite of initiation into manhood?

Yes. Instead of circumcision at age thirteen,

the Jewish people instituted another religious ritual, *bar mitzvah.*

6. What was the nature of God's covenant with Abraham?

The covenant symbolized by *berit milah* is recorded in Genesis 17: "I will be God to you and to your offspring to come. I give the land you sojourn in to you and your offspring to come, all the land of Canaan, as an everlasting possession. I will be their God."

Two other covenant symbols appear in the Torah. One is the rainbow that appeared after the great flood of Noah's time: "When the rainbow appears in the clouds, I will remember My covenant between Me and you and every living creature . . . so that the waters shall never again become a flood to destroy all flesh" (Genesis 9). The second is the Shabbat: "The Israelite people shall keep the Sabbath, observing the Sabbath throughout all ages as a covenant for all time between Me and the people of Israel" (Exodus 31).

Berit milah, then, is one of three major covenant symbols in the first two books of the Torah. It stands as the physical sign of the covenant, while the rainbow is nature's testimony and Shabbat is a communal expression of God's special relationship with the Jewish people.

7. How important is berit milah in Judaism?

With circumcision now fairly common among newborn male babies of all religions, it may be hard to grasp the powerful religious influence it once held and still holds in Judaism. The great Jewish philosopher Spinoza said that "the sign of circumcision is . . . so important . . . it alone would preserve the nation forever," while the Talmud states that "were it not for the blood of the covenant, heaven and earth would not exist."

In biblical times, as we have seen, failure to circumcise a male child resulted in that individual being "cut off" from his people. By the time of Joshua, the Hebrew word *arelim,* or "uncircumcised ones," had become a term applied to "unclean" heathens such as the Philistines. Exodus 4 relates that God was even ready to kill Moses for not circumcising his son Gershom, a tragedy

that was averted when his wife Zipporah performed the act.

By the time of the Babylonian exile (586 B.C.E.), Shabbat and *berit milah* had become the two major symbols of Judaism, so much so that various tyrants, in their attempts to force Jewish assimilation, forbade *berit milah.* In 168 B.C.E., the Assyrian king Antiochus Epiphanes IV tried to abolish *berit milah,* one reason for the Maccabean revolt we recall at Chanukah time. In 132 C.E., the Roman emperor Hadrian made *berit milah* a capital crime. The Jews, however, refused to give it up, many choosing martyrdom rather than surrender. *Berit milah,* then, comes down to us today as a legacy of stubborn adherence to treasured values and religious observance.

8. Did Jews as a group ever move away from berit milah as a religious practice?

No. There were periods in history, however, when circumcision was in some manner challenged. The first instance occurred after the Exodus from Egypt. All the Jews who came out of Egypt were circumcised, but those born in the wilderness were not. The Book of Joshua 5 relates that Joshua arranged for all the Israelites to be circumcised before they entered Canaan, thus preventing the ritual from fading away due to neglect.

The second major challenge to *berit milah* came during Hellenistic times. Many Jewish males wished to compete in the Greek games of that era. Since the participants competed in the nude, spectators could easily distinguish the Jewish contestants. Wanting "to be like everyone else," many Jews underwent a painful operation called an epispasm, which created the impression that the foreskin was intact. The rabbis of the time were so distressed by this practice that they denied a place in the world to come to anyone having the surgery.

Greek culture faded away, but *berit milah* faced a third challenge during the second century C.E. The Roman emperor, Antonius Pius, realizing that the harsh laws of his predecessors would not stop circumcision, decreed a compromise. He declared that Jews could be circumcised but forbade the practice for non-Jews. This seemingly reasonable law had crucial consequences for Jews of that time.

Until that era, Jews had engaged in extensive missionary activity. One of the conditions of conversion, however, was *berit milah*. Pius's law, then, effectively curtailed Jewish proselytism and opened the door for Paul and the Christians, who had dismissed the ceremony as unnecessary, to win many converts who might otherwise have chosen Judaism.

The most recent resistance to *berit milah* came from the Reform Movement. In the mid-nineteenth century, the early Reformers attempted to abolish it as a ritual that had lost meaning in modern times. The power of *berit milah* among the people, however, precluded such an action. After twenty years of debate, a compromise was reached. *Berit milah* was to be encouraged, but the traditional requirement of circumcision as a condition for conversion was eliminated.

Berit milah, then, has survived every challenge put to it for almost forty centuries. The fascinating details of its history are matched by the beauty and power of its religious symbols and ritual.

Berit Milah: Preparations and Participants

After studying the history and significance of *berit milah*, we are now ready to examine its unique preparation and participants.

1. When does berit milah take place?

The ceremony of *berit milah* is celebrated on the eighth day after birth, even if that day falls on Yom Kippur or Shabbat. Of course, *berit milah* may be delayed for reasons of health. In such an instance, very traditional Jews will then circumcise only during the week and not on Shabbat, Yom Kippur, or a Jewish festival. In many hospitals today, male babies are routinely circumcised on the fourth or fifth day after birth. It is, therefore, advisable to tell your doctor that you are Jewish and intend to have a *berit milah* in accordance with Jewish practice.

2. Where should the ceremony be held?

Berit milah may be celebrated in the synagogue, hospital, or home, usually during the morning or daylight hours. Relatively few Jews choose the synagogue option today. Many hospitals have a special room set aside for *berit milah*, and there is no reason to be reluctant about conducting the service in this setting if parents prefer a hospital environment. Still, the home, with the sense of warmth it contributes to this joyous occasion, is the most suitable place for *berit milah*. The great majority of Jews today observe the ritual in their own households.

3. What preparations should be made for the actual day of berit milah?

Most Reform Jews do not make any special preparations for *berit milah*. There are, however, a number of Orthodox customs with which we should be familiar. Many traditional Jews will prepare a feast of fruits and beverages on the erev Shabbat before the *berit*. In addition, there is the

Vachnacht, or *Leil Shimurim,* "the night of watching." This custom, which originated in European Jewish communities, derived in part from Jewish superstitions regarding demons which might harm the infant. Fathers would stay up studying all night the evening before the *berit,* with family and friends coming to the child's bedside to recite the *Shema.* Mothers would sometimes sleep with the ritual knife under their pillows, another symbolic form of protection for the still-vulnerable baby.

Some Jews still observe these practices today, but rarely does one see them in Reform Jewish homes.

4. Who should be invited to the berit milah?

It is appropriate to invite family and friends to share in the happiness of the ceremony. A minimum of ten Jews (the traditional *minyan*) is desirable but not essential.

5. Who performs the circumcision?

According to Jewish law, the father or his representative is responsible for circumcising a male child. At one time, fathers actually circumcised their own sons. Abraham, for example, circumcised both Ishmael and Isaac.

Over the centuries, however, the institution of the *mohel* emerged. The *mohel,* trained in the surgical procedures of *berit milah,* became a professional representative of the fathers of the community. To this day, all Orthodox and most Conservative Jews insist upon retaining a *mohel* to officiate at the *berit,* either with or without a rabbi present. Modern *mohalim,* including Reform *mo-*

halim, physicians certified by the Reform Movement's *Berit Milah* Board, are carefully trained and certified. There is no reason to be concerned, then, about a *mohel's* professional expertise.

Reform Jews ask either a *mohel* or their family physician to perform the circumcision. The physician, when one is used, should be Jewish and may be joined by the leader of the religious ceremony of *berit milah,* whether a rabbi or parent.

6. Who else participates in the ritual?

In Orthodoxy, only males recite the traditional blessings at the *berit milah.* In Reform Judaism, women have equal roles in the ceremony. We have already mentioned the *mohel* or doctor as well as the rabbi or leader of the service. In addition, there are the *sandak, kvatter,* and *kvatterin,* whom we have come to know as the baby's godparents.

7. What do sandak, kvatter, and kvatterin mean?

The word *sandak,* translated as "godfather," derives from a Greek term meaning "one who is with the child" or "patron." *Kvatter* and *kvatterin* are German words, translated as "godfather" and "godmother."

8. When did the institution of godparents originate and what do they do in the ceremony?

Scholars trace the origins of the word *sandak* to the tenth century C.E., with the *kvatter* and *kvatterin* emerging some time later in European countries. These scholars, however, also tell us that the role of the *sandak* was performed many centuries earlier. We know that the *mohel* was assisted by someone, as early as the time of the apostle Paul, who "changed" *berit milah* to Baptism and kept what was to become the *sandak* as an assistant to the priest. Parents would ask a close friend or respected community leader to assume this responsibility, which consisted of assisting the *mohel* during the procedure of circumcision. The *sandak* would sit and hold the infant while the surgical operation was performed. When German Jewry introduced the concept of a *kvatter* and *kvatterin* in addition to the *sandak,* their assumption was that this couple would be copartners with the parents in providing for the child's Jewish upbringing.

Once again we are struck by the genius of the Jewish people who succeeded in transforming the job of a minor functionary in a religious ritual into a lifelong responsibility for the continuity of Judaism. Parents today will usually ask close friends to be godparents to their newborn baby. It is a great honor.

9. Are there any other participants in the ceremony?

A treasured Jewish legend holds that the prophet Elijah is present at every *berit milah.* Elijah, most commonly thought of as the forerunner of the Messianic Age, is also often considered the "angel of the covenant" (*Malachi* 3:1), a protector of little children—in effect, the "guardian angel." Traditional Jews, therefore, set aside a special chair for Elijah at the *berit,* with the baby placed in the chair prior to the circumcision.

Berit Milah and Berit Hachayim: The Ceremony

With the family, friends, rabbi, and *mohel* or doctor in attendance, the actual ritual of *berit milah* is ready to begin.

1. What is the order of the traditional service?
Customarily, two candles are lit in the room where the ceremony is to take place, as a symbol of life and the presence of God. (At one time, the lighted candles very probably were also intended to ward off possible demons that might try to harm the baby.)

 a. The *kvatterin* (godmother) takes the baby from the mother and brings it to the *kvatter* (godfather).

 b. The *kvatter* then enters with the child and everyone stands and says *Baruch haba,* "Blessed be he who comes." This constitutes a welcome to both the infant and the prophet Elijah. In gematria, the Jewish science of numbers, the Hebrew word *haba* (hei-bet-alef) has the numerical equivalent of eight, reflecting, say the rabbis, the eighth day after birth on which the ceremony takes place. In addition, there are those who say that *haba* is an acronym for the phrase *Hinei ba Eliyahu,* "Behold, Elijah comes."

 c. The father of the infant then recites a prescribed reading indicating his acceptance of the responsibility for bringing his son into the covenant, the *berit.*

 d. The *kvatter* or *mohel* places the baby on the special chair for Elijah which has been prepared prior to the ceremony. The infant is then lifted from Elijah's chair and placed upon the knees of the *sandak,* while all others remain standing.

 e. The *mohel* recites the following blessing: *Baruch Atah Adonai Elohenu Melech ha'olam asher kideshanu bemitzvotav vetzivanu al hamilah.* "Blessed are You, O Lord our God, Ruler of the universe, who has made us holy through *mitzvot* and ordained circumcision."

 f. The *mohel* performs the circumcision in three steps: *milah,* the cutting of the foreskin; *periah,* the removal of the underlying membrane; *mezizah,* drawing the blood from the wound. At one time, *milah* was performed with a knife. Today, many *mohalim* use a special surgical clamp which facilitates the operation.

 g. During the circumcision, the father recites the following blessing: *Baruch Atah Adonai Elohenu Melech ha'olam asher kideshanu bemitzvotav vetzivanu lehachniso bevrito shel Avraham avinu.* "Blessed are You, O Lord our God, Ruler of the universe, who has made us holy through *mitzvot* and has commanded us to bring our sons into the covenant of Abraham our father."

 h. All those present recite a prayer expressing the hope that the baby will grow up into a life of study, marriage, and good deeds.

 i. The *mohel* then chants the blessing for the wine and a prayer which gives the baby his Hebrew name. The godfather sips the wine,

and a few drops are also placed on the baby's lips. This concludes the traditional ceremony, although it is quite common to add songs, readings, and poetry. A festive meal traditionally follows.

2. Is there a special Reform ceremony for berit milah?

Yes, the Reform ritual and ceremonies for a host of other home celebrations are included in *Gates of the House*, published by the Central Conference of American Rabbis. The book is a must for every Reform Jewish household.

3. How do you react to those who say that circumcision is a barbaric custom?

That charge was confronted as early as the time of Philo, the brilliant Jewish philosopher of the Greek era. Philo staunchly defended circumcision on hygienic as well as religious grounds. Today, almost 2,000 years later, modern researchers have cast doubt on the long-held assumption that circumcision protects males against cancer of the penis and, in large measure, their wives from cervical cancer as well.

For Jews, though medical benefits would be welcome news, the symbolic entry into the covenant remains the central reason for *berit milah*. It is a religious ceremony, a Jewish ceremony, a ritual that dramatizes the uniqueness of Judaism.

4. What happens if a male baby is circumcised early?

As we have already noted, some hospitals have been known to routinely circumcise babies on the fourth or fifth day after birth. In such an unusual case, Orthodox Jews will perform *Hatafat dam berit,* "the drawing of blood of the covenant," the shedding of a single drop of blood in place of the full ceremony of *berit milah.* Many Reform Jews will often conduct the ceremony of *berit milah,* minus the surgical procedure.

5. What if a child is uncircumcised?

Occasionally, usually for reasons of health, male infants cannot be circumcised within the eight-day period. Jewish law dictates, however, that even an uncircumcised Jew is a full Jew if his mother is Jewish. *Berit milah* should be performed as soon as possible following any delay.

6. Did the ritual objects used in berit milah ever become the objects of artistic creation?

Yes. The *mohel's* surgical instruments and carrying case were frequently finely-crafted and quite elegant in design. The chair of Elijah was often an object of great beauty, carved out of wood or cast in precious metal. The flint knives of Joshua's time and metal knives of the Roman period are today treasured artifacts in many museums.

7. Jesus was Jewish. Did he have a berit milah?

Yes. Since the sixth century, many Christians have marked the eighth day after Jesus' birth as the Feast of the Circumcision of Jesus. We, too, celebrate January 1st—but as our secular New Year's Day!

8. Is there any ceremony like berit milah for baby girls?

Until recently, Judaism had no special home celebration to welcome female infants into the covenant. In Orthodoxy, fathers were given an *aliyah* (the honor of reciting the blessing before and after a section of the weekly Torah portion was read) at the synagogue the first Shabbat after a girl was born. At this time the child also received a Hebrew name. After services, both mother and father were honored at a congregational *kiddush.* In Reform temples, a baby-naming ceremony involving both parents was celebrated most commonly thirty days after the birth. Still, the absence of a special home ritual was disturbing, especially to liberal Jews. A few congregations created their own ceremonies for girls, and the popularity of the idea quickly made it a widespread practice among many Reform and Conservative Jewish families. The CCAR's *Gates of the House* now contains the service of *berit hachayim,* the Covenant of Life. You will want to consider it as an option for your family's newborn girls.

Berit milah and *berit hachayim* are more than ritual, more than symbol. They dramatize the Jewish insistence that each Jew must enter into an *individual* relationship with God, Torah, and the people of Israel. Judaism, unlike some other faiths, is not a religion by proxy. Each one of us counts in strengthening Judaism—for ourselves, our children, and for generations yet to come.

·14·
NAMES

Some Background

Now that we know about the Jewish rituals for naming newborn infants—*berit milah, berit hachayim,* or a special temple ceremony—we ask an even more basic question: where do Jewish names come from, and how do Jewish parents select a name for their child?

1. Are names important in Judaism?

Very much so. From biblical times onward, Jews have always devoted great care to the selection of names. In our Jewish tradition, names can be an expression of individuality, a commemoration of a great life event, a tribute to the dead, or an honor to the living.

2. How did naming begin?

According to Genesis 1:26, God created Adam (derived from the Hebrew, *adamah,* "ground"). Later, after the first woman came into being, Adam called his wife Eve (in Hebrew, *Chavah,* "life") "because she was the mother of all living things" (Genesis 3:20).

Eve named Cain (from the Hebrew, *kinyan,* "acquisition" or "possession") and Abel (in Hebrew, *Hevel,* "vanity"). And so it went, generation by generation, fathers and mothers naming their children on the basis of a variety of criteria.

3. How were names selected in biblical times?

Interestingly, no two people in the Torah have the same given name. Indeed, the same might be said of the entire Bible, with one or two exceptions. Imagine how unique it was to be the only person in the world with your name! Some people were named after birds and animals, like Jonah ("dove"). Some were named after plants or flowers, like Tamar ("palm"). Isaac ("laughter") derived his name from an event: Sarah, his mother, laughed when God's messengers announced that she would bear a child at the age of 90 (Genesis 18:12). And Eve, as we have seen, was named for an idea, the concept of life itself. In biblical times, we find the mother selecting a child's name in almost every instance; the name was given at birth. This practice was modified over the centuries, with both parents gradually coming to choose the name and with the name conferred during the special ceremonies we have already studied.

4. When did Jews begin naming children after other people?

This custom began in the sixth century B.C.E., after the destruction of the First Temple in Jerusalem. By custom, not law, Jews started to name their sons and daughters after close relatives. Ashkenazic Jews named infants only after those who had died, usually grandparents, in the belief that to name a child after a living person might shorten that person's life. Sephardic Jews, on the other hand, often named babies after the living, usually a grandparent or a parent. To the Sephardim, this custom was an expression of great honor and respect. These two naming patterns continue today in Ashkenazic and Sephardic communities around the world.

5. Did a child's name always match that of the relative?

At first, the name chosen was exactly the same as that of the relative. As time went on, however, modern equivalents were often substituted. Jews did not hesitate to adopt names reflective of the culture in which they lived. Moses was an Egyptian name, Mordechai and Esther, Babylonian. The great Jewish philosopher Philo had a Greek name, while the name of the brilliant medieval Jewish scholar Saadia was Arabic.

The rabbis of the talmudic era were concerned that "modern" names might lead to assimilation. In the post-talmudic period, therefore, the custom arose of Jews having two names, one civil, one Hebrew. The civil, or secular, name was the name you were "called by" in your day-to-day life, as well as the name on your civil birth certificate. Your Hebrew name, on the other hand, was used when you were called up to the Torah (an *aliyah*),

"Adam Naming the Creation," a 1900 engraving illustrating Genesis 2:19-20.

when someone prayed for your health (a *misheberach*), and for all other religious documents (such as a *ketubah* or a *get*).

This practice enabled Jews to take more modern given names, to use only the first letter of the deceased or living relative's first name, or, as they chose, to select a biblical name or the actual name of the relative.

6. Did all Jews name children after relatives?

No. As names were a matter of custom rather than Jewish law, the people were free to name their children as they wished. Countless numbers of Jewish children, for example, were named after the sympathetic conqueror, Alexander the Great. Chasidic Jews often gave their children the name of their revered rebbe. Jewish values became names, as in Shalom or Shelomo. And, for those who dreamed of a return to the land of our ancestors, their children were given the names of sites in Eretz Yisrael, such as Sharon (as in Sharon Valley). The children bore living testimony to their eternal hope of returning to the land. On the other hand, some families named *exclusively* after departed relatives. Scholars enjoy pointing to the family of the great Jewish teacher, Hillel, where only four male names (Hillel, Simon, Gamaliel, and Judah) were used in fourteen generations, spanning some 500 years!

7. When did Jews begin to use last names?

With few exceptions, not until the eighteenth century. Before that time, a child was identified as *x ben* (son of) or *bat* (daughter of) *y* (the father's Hebrew first name). Thus, Daniel ben Mosheh was Daniel the son of Moses, and Tsiporah bat Yosef was Tsiporah the daughter of Joseph. We see this practice illustrated in the Bible in the person of Joshua bin (ben) Nun, Joshua the son of Nun.

After the destruction of the Second Temple (70 C.E.), Jews moved into many different societies, with the word for "son" or "daughter" changing with the host country. When Jews spoke Aramaic (beginning second century C.E.), the formula was *x bar y*, as in Bar Kochba. It is from the Aramaic that we also get the term *bar mitzvah*, or "son of the commandment." In Arabic-speaking lands, the word "son" was "ibn," hence names like Solomon ibn Gabirol, Solomon the son of Gabirol.

Because this custom often resulted in very long names, some Jews were referred to by acronyms consisting of the first initials of their names. The most famous of these was Rambam for *Rabbi Moses ben Maimon*. Note that the title of Rabbi was added to the beginning of the name, while the religious status of the individual, if a *kohen* (descendant of the Temple priests) or a Levite (descendant of the Temple assistants to the *kohen*), was appended at the end as *hakohen* or Halevi.

8. Why was the eighteenth century a turning point?

About the time of the French Revolution, most European countries passed laws ordering all Jews to take surnames. In many instances, this was a device to promote assimilation of the Jews into modern society, the age of enlightenment having freed them from the ghetto and granted them a measure of equality. For a great number of Jews, selecting a family name was a simple matter. A Hebrew name such as Avraham ben Yosef became Abraham Josephson, or Moses ben Mendel

became Moses Mendelssohn. Other Jews took the name of the city or country in which they lived, resulting in family names like Warschauer (Warsaw), Berliner, and Hollander. One's religious status sometimes became a last name, as with Cohen or Levy. And professions were also used, like Cantor, Singer, Lehrer (teacher), or Goldsmith.

In some countries, however, the imposition of surnames served as an opportunity for anti-Semitic hatred to find expression. Jews were often forced to take demeaning names, like Fresser (glutton). A few countries prohibited Jews from using Jewish names altogether, while the Nazis selected 279 "special" names reserved for Jews alone. These included the names of ancient Jewish persecutors, Ahab, Moab, and Jezebel, and names expressing contempt, like *chamor* (donkey). Occasionally, the origin of a family name reflected a touching story. Such was the case with a Scandinavian Jewish man, whose beloved wife, Henya, had recently died. When the government enacted a law requiring the adoption of surnames, he decided to make his family name a memorial to his life-partner. Thus the name Hendin came into being.

Over the past 4,000 years, our customs and practices regarding given and family names have undergone much change.

Names: Some Jewish Teachings, Superstitions, and Favorites

We have examined how names came into being, some of the ways in which Jews selected names for their children, and the historical events leading to adoption by Jews of last names. In terms of Jewish teachings, however, the ultimate attainment in life is a good name, a respected name.

1. How do Jewish teachings reflect this position?

Consider these five statements, two from the Bible, two from the midrashic literature, and one from the Mishnah:

a. "A good name is preferable to great riches" (Proverbs 22:1).

b. "A good name is better than fine oil" (Ecclesiastes 7:1).

c. "The earned name is worth much more than the given name" (*Ecclesiastes Rabbah*).

d. "Every person has three names: one parents give them, one others call them, and one they acquire themselves" (*Ecclesiastes Rabbah*).

e. "There are three crowns, the crown of the Torah, the crown of priesthood, and the crown of royalty, but the crown of a good name excels them all" (*Pirke Avot*).

It is no accident that the founder of Chasidism was called the Baal Shem Tov (Master of the

Good Name) or that God is sometimes referred to merely as Hashem (The Name). A Jewish name, then, was far more than a label; by striving to make it a good name, the Jew aimed at transforming it into a badge of honor.

2. Did our ancestors ever change their names?

Yes, and for different reasons. In the Torah, two stories in particular illustrate how a change of name reflected a change in character. During his early years, Abram (father of Aram) moved toward monotheism and leadership of the Jewish people. Later in life, God changed his name to Abraham (father of a multitude of nations), a change of name as a reward for a lifetime of service to God. Jacob (heel grasper) stole his brother Esau's birthright, deceived his father, Isaac, and had to leave home as a result. Later in life, however, after wrestling with the angel (or some say his identity), he became Israel (champion of God), the father of the twelve tribes of Israel, and the progenitor of the Jewish people.

3. How are names connected with superstitions?

Throughout Jewish history, names were viewed as having special power. Accordingly, many superstitions grew up around names, especially during the Middle Ages. Some Jews had secret names, which they would not reveal to anyone. Other Jews refused to marry a person who had the same name as their mother or father, and would even hesitate to live in the same town as an individual bearing their name. All of these customs derived in large measure from a fear that the Angel of Death might confuse two people of the same name, leading to the premature demise of one or the other.

To further "confuse" the Angel of Death, Jewish families often took unusual steps in selecting names. In Poland, in a household where several young people had died, babies would sometimes receive names indicative of advanced years, such as Alter (old) or Zaida (grandfather). A custom followed by some Jews, even in modern times, is that of changing the name of a person who is near death. In accordance with talmudic, rabbinic, and mystical traditions, the individual is given a name such as Chaim (life) or its female equivalent, Chayah.

4. What are some good biblical and modern Israeli names for children?

As we have seen, modern Jews will employ a variety of criteria in selecting names for their children, and no list of names could possibly be complete. Here, however, in no particular order, is a list of personal favorites and their English meanings. For your own selections, you may want to consult one of the many books of Jewish names, available in your temple gift shop or local Jewish bookstore.

For Boys
Adam (humankind, man); Ari (lion); Benjamin (Binyamin, son of my right hand); Daniel (God is my judge); David (beloved); Jonathan (Yonatan, God has given); Joshua (Yehoshuah, God is my salvation); Michael (Who is like God?); Micah (Michah, Who is like God?); Noah (Noach, rest, quiet); Zechariah or Zachariah (remembrance of the Lord).

For Girls
Ariella (lioness of God); Aviva (spring); Dahlia (bough); Deborah (Devorah, bee); Elana (tree); Leora (light); Michal (Who is like God?); Naomi (pleasant); Rachel (ewe); Sarah (princess); Shira (song); Tamar (palm tree).

Interestingly, in recent years, biblical names have become more popular with young Jewish parents. It is yet another demonstration of the growing relationship between our people and our past.

·15·

RITES OF PASSAGE

Pidyon Haben: Redemption of the First-Born Son

1. What is the meaning of pidyon haben?

Pidyon haben (literally, "Redemption of the First-Born Son") refers to a traditional Jewish ritual that originated in ancient times. While most Orthodox and many Conservative Jews observe *pidyon haben* today, it is practiced in very few Reform households. Still, the history of the ritual and the Jewish values it embodies are worthy of our attention.

2. What is the basis of pidyon haben?

The ceremony of *pidyon haben* derives from a series of biblical passages which portray God as laying claim to the first-born of both animals and human beings. Exodus 22:28–29 sets forth the command clearly: "The first-born of thy sons shalt thou give unto Me. Likewise shalt thou do with thine oxen and with thy sheep."

The practical interpretation of this injunction led to the practice of dedicating all first-born things to God by bringing them to the *kohanim*, the priests. First-born animals were offered as special sacrifices, while first-born sons entered the priesthood or priestly service.

3. Does the Torah indicate why God would demand such a course of action?

Numbers 3:13 establishes a link between the dedication of the first-born and the Exodus from Egypt. You will recall that the last of the ten plagues involved the death of every Egyptian first-born son. The first-born sons of Hebrews, however, were spared, or "passed over," an act of divine beneficence we recall at the Pesach seder. The passage from Numbers declares: "On the day that I smote all the first-born in the land of Egypt, I hallowed unto Me all the first-born in Israel, both man and beast, Mine they shall be."

In saving these first-born sons, then, the Torah indicates, God consecrated these children to service in the Temple in Jerusalem. Indeed, the Talmud says that, until the Sanctuary was built in Jerusalem, the *kohanim* were exclusively first-born sons.

4. How was the redemption accomplished?

The original ceremony of *pidyon haben* took place one month after birth. First-born children who were male and were not children of *kohanim* or Levites were symbolically released from serving in the priesthood through payment of five shekels of silver to one of the priests. The money was used to sustain the Temple, and parents returned to their homes with their offspring.

5. Didn't pidyon haben become anachronistic after the destruction of the Temple?

Yes. In fact, rabbis in the Middle Ages attempted to let the ritual fade into obscurity. As is so often the case, however, the symbolic power of the practice among the people as well as its perceived divine origin prevented them from abolishing it entirely. Instead, the rabbis greatly limited those who required *pidyon haben*. In addition to the accepted practice of exempting sons of fathers who were *kohanim* or Levites, the rabbis also excluded children of women whose fathers fell into one of these two categories. Also released from this obligation were first-born sons delivered by Caesarean section and sons following a miscarriage after the third month of a woman's first pregnancy. Reform Judaism discouraged the practice altogether, though a number of Reform Jews choose to observe it today.

6. According to tradition, who requires pidyon haben?

The commonly accepted definition is that *peter rechem*, the "son that opens the womb," is to be redeemed, so long as the child survives for thirty days.

A son born naturally after the mother had previously given birth by a Caesarean section is obligated, even if the actual first child is a male. Also included are sons delivered in a pregnancy after the first pregnancy has miscarried during the first forty days. If a man marries twice, the first-born son of each wife must be redeemed.

7. When and where does pidyon haben take place?

The ceremony is held on the thirtieth day following birth. If the thirtieth day falls on Shabbat, a fast day, or a festival, the ceremony is delayed for twenty-four hours. The ritual is a home celebration, and family and friends are usually invited to take part.

8. What is the order of the traditional pidyon haben ritual?

a. The father hands his son to a *kohen*, who symbolically represents the ancient priesthood.

b. The father recites a formula in Hebrew meaning: "This is my first-born son. He is the first-born of his mother, and the Holy One, blessed be He, has commanded us to redeem him."

c. The *kohen* asks the father: "Which would you rather do—give me your first-born son, the first-born of his mother, or redeem him for five shekels, as you are obligated to give according to the Torah?"

d. The father responds: "I prefer to redeem my son. And here is his redemption price, which I must give according to the Torah."

e. The father then gives the *kohen* a sum of money, usually $5.00. The *kohen* takes the money and hands the baby back to his father.

f. The father recites two *berachot*, one regarding the *mitzvah* of *pidyon haben*, the other the *Shehecheyanu*.

g. The *kohen* places the money on the child's head and says: "This for that, this in commutation of that, this in remission of that." He then invokes a blessing, wishing the child a life filled with Torah, a happy marriage, and performance of good deeds. The priestly benediction and the *kiddush* then conclude the ceremony.

9. Is there any ceremony for the redemption of daughters?

In recent years, some couples have created personal rituals for their first-born daughters that are parallel to *pidyon haben*.

As we have already noted, Reform Judaism formally moved away from *pidyon haben* as a meaningful ceremony for modern times. Nevertheless, its symbolic significance, as an expression of thanks to God for a child, and its ties to the history of our people make it an appropriate subject of study for us all. In the final analysis, nothing in the Jewish experience is inherently foreign to us as Jews, and the more we learn, the more we can appreciate our uniqueness as members of the Reform community.

Bar/Bat Mitzvah: Some Historical Background

1. What is the meaning of bar/bat mitzvah?

Bar and *bat mitzvah* mean, literally, "son and daughter of the Commandment." *Bat mitzvah* is Hebrew, while *bar mitzvah*, historically a much earlier ceremony, is Aramaic. The word *bar* is the Aramaic equivalent of the Hebrew, *ben*.

2. What event do bar and bat mitzvah mark in Jewish life?

Historically, first *bar mitzvah* and later *bat mitzvah* represented a ceremonial recognition that a young person had reached the age when he or she was responsible for the performance of the *mitzvot*. The individual was then no longer a minor according to Jewish law and, thereby, took on new religious privileges and responsibilities. For boys, this age was thirteen, for girls, twelve.

3. What is the origin of bar mitzvah?

The beginnings of *bar mitzvah* are obscure. It is not mentioned in the Torah, nor is there any biblical indication that thirteen was the age at which one attained religious majority. We do know that many ancient civilizations conducted tribal initiations for young males at the age of thirteen, corresponding with the onset of puberty. These rites often included painful ordeals, such as circumcision. Indeed, Abraham's son Ishmael was circumcised at thirteen. However, Judaism recast circumcision in a religious context and moved it to the age of eight days as *berit milah*, a formal ritual of welcoming male babies into the Covenant between God and Israel.

Most scholars feel that the association between age thirteen and mandated religious observance began during the Second Temple period (between 516 B.C.E. and 70 C.E.). A section of the Babylonian Talmud (second or third century C.E.) affirms that "until the thirteenth year, it is the father's duty to raise his son." After that, however, he must say "Blessed be He who has removed from me the responsibility for this boy!" In addition, *Pirke Avot* 5:24 states that at age thirteen a boy is responsible for the *mitzvot*.

In ancient times, a father would take his son to the Temple in Jerusalem to receive a blessing. The *kohen* would also offer a prayer expressing the hope that the boy would learn Torah and live a happy life of good deeds. At that point in life, the young man was eligible to be counted as a member of the *minyan* (quorum of Jews required for prayer) and could also then buy and sell property and make binding vows.

4. This doesn't sound like the bar mitzvah ceremony we recognize.

That's correct. The *bar mitzvah* ceremony was developed as a public recognition of a legal and religious status, attained with or without the ritual. In other words, a Jewish boy of thirteen years and one day automatically became a *bar mitzvah* even if no public ceremony took place.

While the beginnings of "our" *bar mitzvah* ceremony appeared as early as the sixth century C.E., it was not until the Middle Ages that a fully developed ritual emerged. By the thirteenth or fourteenth century, the custom of calling a boy up to the Torah was established as the way of recognizing entry into manhood. The *bar mitzvah* boy would chant the blessings, all or part of the Torah portion of the week, and/or the haftarah section from the prophetic books. The boy's father would then recite a special blessing: *Baruch shepetarani me'onsho shel zeh.* "Blessed is He who has freed me from responsibility for this boy." The *bar mitzvah* boy would often give a scholarly address on the *sidrah* or some section of the Talmud. Then followed a gala feast, called *seudat mitzvah* ("meal of celebrating the performance of a *mitzvah*"), to which family, friends, and sometimes the entire Jewish community would be invited. In short, then, almost all the elements we associate with the modern *bar mitzvah* ceremony were present by the Middle Ages.

5. When did bat mitzvah begin?

Starting in the second or third century C.E., Jewish girls at age twelve took on legal responsibility for the performance of the *mitzvot.* As with age thirteen for boys, twelve probably corresponded with their onset of puberty. However, girls were subject to far fewer commandments than boys. Since Jewish society at that time saw females solely as mothers and housewives, women were exempted from a whole series of time-bound commandments, on the assumption that their work

and presence in the home took precedence. Today, liberal Jews affirm the total equality of women in terms of religious privileges and responsibilities.

Many centuries passed before any *bat mitzvah* ceremony appeared. In the 1800s, Reform Judaism abolished *bar mitzvah* in favor of Confirmation for both boys and girls (*bat mitzvah* not considered an option at that time). Within the nineteenth-century traditional community, some families held a *seudat mitzvah* for a daughter on her twelfth birthday, with the girl sometimes delivering a talk and her father reciting the *"Baruch Shepetarani."*

The first-known *bat mitzvah* in North America, of Judith Kaplan, daughter of Mordecai Kaplan, was held in 1921. Dr. Kaplan, founder of the Reconstructionist movement, scheduled his daughter's *bat mitzvah* on a Friday night. Judith recited the *berachah*, read a section from her *chumash* (not the Torah scroll itself) and its English translation, then recited the concluding *berachah.* *Bat mitzvah* was born. Reform (which had by this time reintroduced *bar mitzvah*) and then Conservative congregations quickly adopted *bat mitzvah*, though in slightly different forms.

Celebrating Bar/Bat Mitzvah

1. At what age do bar and bat mitzvah take place?

In all branches of Judaism, *bar mitzvah* is usually celebrated on the first Shabbat after the boy's thirteenth birthday. Occasionally, *bar mitzvah* is marked at a somewhat later date, to enable family and friends to be present.

Few, if any, Orthodox congregations have a formal *bat mitzvah* ceremony. In Conservative congregations where *bat mitzvah* is celebrated, it is marked at either age twelve or thirteen. In Reform temples, girls, like boys, mark symbolic entry into Jewish adulthood at age thirteen.

2. Are bar/bat mitzvahs always held on Shabbat?

No. We recall that the public recognition of one's attaining Jewish religious majority involves

being called up to the *bimah* to chant or recite the *berachot* over the Torah and/or the *berachot* before and after the Haftarah (a selection from the Bible's prophetic books). Since the Torah may be read on Monday, Thursday, or Shabbat, *bar/bat mitzvah* celebrations are currently observed on all of these days.

In Conservative congregations, *bar mitzvah* is usually held on Shabbat morning, while *bat mitzvah* is often held on Friday night. Girls may read from the Torah or, alternatively, chant the *berachot* before and after the Haftarah, as well as the Haftarah itself. In Reform temples, boys and girls participate in the service in the same way.

3. What does the Reform bar/bat mitzvah do in the service?

Depending on the congregation, boys and girls may conduct all or part of the service, chant or recite the Torah and/or Haftarah *berachot*, read

or chant the *berachot* over the Torah (an *aliyah*), read a section from the *sidrah* for that week, read or chant the *berachot* for the Haftarah, and read a section from the Haftarah.

4. What does aliyah mean?

The Hebrew word *aliyah* (literally, "going up") is used as a description of being "called up" to read from the Torah. Interestingly, *aliyah* is also the word used to describe the act of immigration to Israel. In Jewish tradition, as far back as biblical times, going to Israel was always referred to as "going up." Leaving Israel, on the other hand, was always described as "going down," as in Israel's "going down into Egypt" in ancient times.

5. Are there times besides bar/bat mitzvah when Jews are called up to the Torah for an aliyah?

In Reform Judaism, any adult member of the congregation may be called up to the Torah for an *aliyah* at any Torah service. It is common practice in all branches of Judaism to mark with an *aliyah* occasions such as the birth of a child, an impending marriage, or recovery from an illness.

6. Are bar and bat mitzvah always celebrated in the synagogue?

While most families consider the synagogue the most meaningful, appropriate, and moving setting for a *bar/bat mitzvah*, there has been experimentation with other settings.

In recent years, growing numbers of families have chosen to travel to Israel to celebrate their *simchah* at the Western Wall in Jerusalem. Should you decide that this is a desirable option, be sure to contact the proper Israeli authorities far in advance. They will give you a date and the section of the Torah to be prepared. The two major drawbacks to this setting are: first, it is available only to boys; second, the moment must usually be shared with other youths. Still, it can be a powerful Jewish experience and should be considered as a possibility.

7. How far in advance should my son or daughter begin to prepare for bar or bat mitzvah?

For *bar/bat mitzvah* to be both a meaningful and substantive Jewish moment, it is essential that it be based on far more than a one-year crash program of study. Four years in the religious/Hebrew school prior to *bar/bat mitzvah* is recommended as a minimum of requisite Jewish education, along with a commitment to continue through twelfth grade after the ceremony.

8. What should we do about a party?

The *bar/bat mitzvah* "party" derives from the custom of serving a *seudat mitzvah* ("meal celebrating the performance of a *mitzvah*") which arose in the Middle Ages. As early as the thirteenth century, local Jewish communities were concerned that such feasts might become ostentatious and wasteful displays of wealth, thereby detracting from the ceremony's religious significance. Accordingly, community leaders often enacted formal legislation, strict guidelines, or special taxes to limit the size and nature of these feasts.

While the custom of each congregation most often dictates the form of *bar/bat mitzvah* parties, more Jewish families today invest the celebration with deeper Jewish feeling. Israeli dancing and singing, for example, are evident more than ever. Jews love *simchahs* and celebrations with family and friends, and now that joy is being shared in ever more Jewish ways.

9. What if you never had a bar/bat mitzvah?

It's never too late. Whether you're sixteen or

sixty, if you want a *bar/bat mitzvah*, you should have one. Many UAHC camps make provisions for teenage *bar/bat mitzvah* training. Numerous UAHC congregations have created adult *bar/bat mitzvah* programs for individual or group instruction. As a result, rabbis throughout the country have reported *bar/bat mitzvah* services for members well into their eighties. If you did not have a *bar/bat mitzvah* and you're prepared to undertake the necessary study, speak to your rabbi. It can be one of the most fulfilling experiences of your adult life.

10. What is the significance of bar/bat mitzvah?

That's a personal question; answers will vary from individual to individual. I personally believe that this Jewish moment constitutes an affirmation of the values upon which the future of our people depends: Jewish study, accomplishment, family, community, and faith. A midrash tells us that at age thirteen Abraham smashed his father's idols

and became the first Jew. One could say that every *bar/bat mitzvah* constitutes a symbolic rebirth of Judaism, the creation of a new Jewish soul, filled with promise yet to be realized.

Confirmation

1. What is Confirmation?

Confirmation is a Reform-originated ceremony for boys and girls, tied to Shavuot, constituting an individual and group affirmation of commitment to the Jewish people.

2. How did Confirmation originate?

Confirmation, one of the "youngest" Jewish life cycle ceremonies, began less than 200 years ago. Most scholars attribute the creation of Confirmation to Israel Jacobson, a wealthy German businessman and a nominal "father" of Reform Judaism.

In 1810, expending more than $100,000 of his own money, Jacobson built a new synagogue in Seesen, Germany. He introduced a number of then-radical reforms, including the use of an organ

and mixed male-female seating. Jacobson felt that *bar mitzvah* was an outmoded ceremony. Accordingly, when five thirteen-year-old boys were about to graduate from the school he maintained, Jacobson designed a new graduation ceremony, held in the school rather than the synagogue. In this manner, Confirmation came into being.

3. So Confirmation was originally only for boys?

Yes. At first only boys were confirmed, usually on the Shabbat of their *bar mitzvah*. Because of the controversial nature of the Confirmation ceremony, the earliest rituals were held exclusively in homes or in schools. In 1817, the synagogue in Berlin introduced a separate Confirmation program for girls. In 1822, the first class of boys and girls was confirmed, a practice that became almost universal in a relatively brief period of time. Slowly, Confirmation moved into the synagogue and began to take shape as we know it today.

4. When was Confirmation tied to the holiday of Shavuot?

Beginning as a simple graduation ceremony and then as a substitute for *bar mitzvah*, Confirmation gradually became a temple-based ritual, held on either the Shabbat of Pesach or of Chanukah. In 1831, Rabbi Samuel Egers of Brunswick, Germany determined to hold Confirmation on Shavuot, the festival of the giving of the Torah at Mt. Sinai. Egers saw a powerful spiritual potential in associating the affirmation of faith by young Jews with the most significant historical faith affirmation of the Jewish people. Egers, then, effected a synthesis between antiquity and modernity, cemented the bond between Shavuot and Confirmation, and invested both with a new spiritual dimension.

5. When did Confirmation come to North America?

The first recorded Confirmation in North America was held at New York's Anshe Chesed Congregation in 1846. Two years later, New York's Congregation Emanu-El adopted Confirmation. The ceremony grew in popularity and, in 1927, the Central Conference of American Rabbis recommended Confirmation as a Movement-wide practice.

6. How did Orthodoxy react to Confirmation?

Many traditionalists opposed Confirmation on the grounds that it represented a move away from tradition and a step towards assimilation. Such opposition often took the form of successful appeals to governmental authorities for suppression of the new ceremony, as seen in the banning of Confirmation in Prussia (1836) and Bavaria (1838). Nevertheless, Confirmation gradually became entrenched as a major life cycle event in Reform Jewish communities. In Europe and North America, *bar* and then *bat mitzvah* reasserted themselves, and Confirmation moved to the ninth and tenth grades.

7. What was the early Confirmation ritual like?

At its inception, Confirmation reflected a graduation motif. After a specified period of study, students were subject to a public examination. The following day, in the rabbi's presence, students uttered personal confessions of faith. The rabbi addressed the class, recited a prayer, and then blessed them. It was a simple service with no fixed ritual.

As Confirmation moved into the synagogue and as its ties to Shavuot strengthened, the ceremony became more elaborate. In the early 1900s, Confirmation took on an air of great pageantry, boys and girls wearing robes, bringing flower offerings to the *bimah*, and participating in dramatic readings and cantatas illustrating themes of dedication and commitment to Judaism. Preparation for Confirmation still included a period of study, but public tests and confessions of faith gave way to more normative exams and papers, and speeches reflecting a deeper understanding of Jewish teachings and values.

In recent decades, Confirmation has lost some of its former pomp and ceremony. Wide variations exist in congregational practice, from an elaborate temple service to a private individual ceremony with the rabbi. Many Confirmation classes undertake social action projects as part of their year of preparation. While tenth-grade Confirmation remains the norm in Reform Judaism, a number

of temples now mark the event in ninth, eleventh, or even twelfth grade. And, since the 1970s, adult Confirmation programs exist in many UAHC congregations. Large numbers of Conservative congregations and some Orthodox synagogues hold Confirmation ceremonies as well.

8. Why would Jews need to "confirm" their faith?

According to Jewish law, if one is born a Jew or converts to Judaism, no further "proof" of membership in the Jewish people is required. The ceremony of Confirmation, then, is not a "requirement," but an opportunity to follow in the footsteps of our ancestors; Moses, Joshua, Josiah, and others "rediscovered" their Jewish roots at different times in their lives. So do our youths stand before the congregation as the ancient Israelites stood at Sinai, recommitting themselves to a people as old as the Torah, and as modern as today.

·16·

THE JEWISH WEDDING

Some Biblical History

1. When did marriage originate?

According to the Torah, the institution of marriage began with Adam and Eve. The Book of Genesis portrays God as saying: "It is not good that man should be alone. . . . Therefore shall a man leave his father and his mother and shall cleave unto his wife, and they shall be one flesh" (Genesis 2:18, 24). One midrash indicates that God personally officiated at Adam and Eve's wedding, thus emphasizing Judaism's high regard for marriage and family life. It is also of interest to note that, of the 613 *mitzvot* (commandments) found in the Torah, the very first (Genesis 1:28) declares: "Be fruitful, and multiply, and replenish the earth. . . ," a clear indication of the value placed upon the bearing and raising of children after marriage.

2. Did the ancients have a wedding ceremony?

Not as we know it. Most scholars agree that "marriages" originally constituted a man's "reserving" a particular woman or women as his property. This was accomplished simply by bringing a woman into his tent or cave (or palace) and having sexual relations with her. As such, it was referred to as "taking a wife." By the time of the Bible, however, the Jewish people had already begun to invest the man/woman relationship with far more than sexual significance. A series of customs arose which laid the groundwork for Judaism's elevation of marriage to a status of great legal and religious significance.

3. What were some of these biblical customs?

a. Arranged marriages.
b. The bride price.
c. Forbidden marriages.
d. Monogamy/polygamy.
e. Rights of the wife.

4. Who arranged marriages?

In biblical times, fathers usually arranged marriages for their children. While romantic love was not unknown (Jacob for Rachel) it was not as central to marriage as it has become today. Accordingly, fathers—or their surrogates—sought out appropriate mates for their sons and daughters. Abraham's servant, Eliezer, for example, was dispatched to find a wife for Isaac (Genesis 24:1—4), and Laban had to give his permission for Jacob to marry Rachel (Genesis 29:15—19). While there were numerous exceptions to this general pattern, the practice, centuries later, gradually blossomed into the institution of the *shadchan* (matchmaker), as we shall see.

5. What was the bride price?

Since women were valuable workers in the

households of the biblical period, any man wishing to marry a woman paid money or property to the woman's father as a form of compensation. Or, alternatively, as in the case of Jacob, a prospective bridegroom worked for his father-in-law for a specified period of time. Over the centuries, the bride price often became a symbolic amount, usually used to help purchase the woman's trousseau.

6. What sorts of marriages were considered forbidden?

In biblical times, severe taboos were attached to a number of marriage categories, foremost among them those involving blood relations. Incest was forbidden in Judaism long before more modern legal systems legislated against such unions (Leviticus 18, 20:17). Marriage to cousins, however, was fairly frequent. Isaac and Rebekah were cousins, as were Jacob and Leah and Rachel. Biblical law strictly forbade marriage to the Canaanites, undying enemies of the Hebrews. It frowned as well on unions with men and women of six other nations (Deuteronomy 7:1–3). These Torah verses, root of the traditional Jewish position against intermarriage, resulted in the Hebrews being basically endogamous.

It is important to recognize, however, that the ban was motivated by religious rather than ethnic or racial considerations: "For they will turn away your children from following Me, that they may serve other gods" (Deuteronomy 7:4).

Accordingly, aside from the Canaanites, the ancient Hebrews were permitted to marry outside of their people *if* their mate embraced Judaism. According to rabbinic literature, Moses' wife Zipporah was a convert. Boaz married Ruth, born a Moabite, who chose Judaism and became the ancestor of King David. A number of Israelite kings married non-Jewish women of royal families in an attempt to forge alliances with foreign powers. In general, however, biblical society emphasized "in-group" marriage.

Special restrictions regarding marriage were placed on the *kohanim*, the priestly class. Owing to his special status, the *kohen* could not marry a harlot or a divorcée (Leviticus 21:7). In addition, the high priest was also prohibited from marrying a widow. He could only marry a virgin (Leviticus

21:14). Other laws protected the dignity of a divorced woman. Once divorced, a man and wife could not remarry each other, if they had married and divorced again. Finally, a man could not marry his wife's sister during his wife's lifetime, even after a divorce (Leviticus 18:18 and Shulchan Aruch).

7. Were the ancient Hebrews all monogamous?

No. Abraham had three wives (Sarah, Hagar, and later, after Sarah's death, Keturah), Jacob two (Leah and Rachel), while King Solomon had 700 wives and 300 concubines! So polygamy was permitted. Only men could have more than one mate, however. A woman was permitted only one husband at a time.

But, though polygamy was allowed, it was prevalent almost solely among the rich. Because of the rights of the bride as articulated in the Torah, only those of substance could afford more than one mate. Most of the prophets discouraged polygamy, pointing to the symbolic "marriage" of God and Israel as the ideal monogamous model for a man and a woman. The practice slowly disappeared among Ashkenazic Jews, though it was not until the year 1040 C.E. that Rabbenu Gershom, a great Jewish scholar, issued a ruling that formally ended polygamy among the Ashkenazim. Among Sephardic and Oriental Jews, the practice continued until relatively recent times—and still is in evidence in countries such as Yemen.

8. Did married women have rights?

Yes. Exodus 21:10 clearly specifies that a husband cannot deny a wife food, clothing, and sex. This verse served as the basis for a whole body of law regarding women's marital rights in talmudic and modern times, as we shall see.

The biblical institution of levirate marriage also served to protect a childless widow. In the event that a man died, leaving no heirs, his wife could have been left destitute, since wives could not lay claim to more than a fraction of their husbands' estates. Therefore, the man's brother was legally obligated to marry the widow, care for her, and hopefully sire children who would perpetuate the family name. A man who refused to perform this obligation had to endure public humiliation through a ceremony known as *chalitzah* (release) (Deuteronomy 25:5–10). Such a ceremony is recorded in the Book of Ruth, Chapters 3 and 4, and is still practiced today in Orthodox communities in Israel and elsewhere.

By the end of the biblical period, then, Jewish marriage was already sanctified and regulated by laws. It had begun to take on the shape, substance, and values of a religious and legal act.

The Jewish Wedding: Some Talmudic Background

By talmudic times (the first five centuries of the Common Era), the Jewish wedding had acquired many layers of ritual in addition to those practiced in biblical society. Furthermore, marriage practices had begun, at least in embryonic fashion, to resemble the modern wedding ceremony.

1. How important was marriage in talmudic times?

The rabbis viewed marriage and child-rearing as primary obligations of every Jew. From their perspective, as we have already seen, the duty to "be fruitful and multiply" was a divine command. Accordingly, many talmudic passages reflect the emphasis placed upon the institution:

"God waits impatiently for man to marry."
"One who does not marry dwells without blessing and without goodness."
"No man without woman, no woman without man, and neither without God."

2. At what age did people get married?

The Talmud suggests the age of eighteen as the ideal time for marriage. There are, however, references to individuals who wed as early as their early teens.

3. How did people get married?

By talmudic times, the process of acquiring a spouse was far more formal and ceremonial than in the Bible. Basically, there were two parts to the ritual: *kiddushin/erusin* and *nissuin*. The first, *kiddushin* (consecration) or *erusin* (betrothal), was equivalent to formalizing an engagement. *Kiddushin/erusin* was effected in one of three ways:

a. *Kesef* (literally, "money")
The formal exchange of an object of value, worth at least a *perutah*, the "penny" of antiquity. This practice, performed in the presence of two witnesses, eventually led to the modern custom of exchanging rings.

b. *Shetar* (literally, "document")
The signing of a legal document in the presence of two witnesses. This document, the *ketubah*, testified to the couple's marriage and specified the bride's rights in the event of a dissolution of the engagement or marriage, or in the event of her spouse's death.

c. *Biah* (literally, "intercourse")
While the Talmud is quite explicit in designating cohabitation as one means of betrothal, it was frowned upon and discouraged by the rabbis. They could not abolish it, as it had its origin in the Torah, and therefore had to be treated as divinely commanded. Social pressures, however, as well as legal measures, sometimes as harsh as flogging, gradually eliminated this practice almost entirely.

4. How long was the engagement?

Through *kiddushin/erusin*, a woman became *arusah*, betrothed. As such, neither she nor her fiancé could contemplate marrying another person without a formal, legal Jewish divorce (*get*). The engagement lasted one year, during which time the bride assembled her trousseau. The marriage was then consummated through the ritual *nissuin* (literally, "elevation"). Today, there is no such prescribed engagement period, *erusin* and *nissuin* having been combined into a single ceremony in about the twelfth century.

5. What was nissuin?

In a sophisticated ritualization of biblical practice, the wife was escorted to her husband's house in a rite which later became ceremonialized as the *chupah* ("marriage canopy"). This ritual sealed the wedding pact.

6. Were there forbidden marriages in the Talmud?

Yes. In addition to the prohibitions delineated in the Torah that we have already studied, the Talmud explicitly forbids Jewish weddings involving certain individuals, among them:

a. Minors: boys under 13 years of age, girls under the age of 12.

b. Eunuchs, as they would be unable to fulfill the *mitzvah* of having children.

c. Deaf and dumb men and women, unless they could use sign language to make clear that they understood the legal and contractual obligations of marriage.

d. The incompetent, since they could not be assumed to comprehend and accept the legal obligations of marriage.

Furthermore, the Talmud forbids marriage between:

a. A man and his former wife (if she had been married to another man in the interim).

b. A woman and the man who represented her in her divorce proceedings.

c. A woman and the only witness to her husband's death.

d. A Jew and a *mamzer* (child of a forbidden marriage).

e. A Jew and a *shetuki* (person of unknown parentage).

Special restrictions were placed on second or third marriages. A widower had to observe a thirty-day mourning period before marrying again. A widow or female divorcée had to wait ninety days after being widowed or divorced so that, if she was pregnant at the time, the paternity of the child could be determined. Also, if a widow or divorcée had an infant, she could not remarry until the baby reached two years of age. Finally, if a woman had two husbands who died from other than natural causes or accident, she was banned from ever remarrying.

7. Were marriages still arranged in talmudic times?

Yes, by all means. While the institution of the *shadchan* (matchmaker) had not yet come to full flower, parents busily sought to find the best prospective mate for their children. Where a *shadchan* was involved, he/she received a fee and a percentage of the dowry. The rabbis offered guidance as to how to evaluate a possible "intended," directing their counsel to the male-dominated society in which they lived. Though clearly some of their advice is inappropriate today, it gives us a glimpse into the rabbinic mind:

a. Marry the daughter of a learned man.

b. Marry a woman of the same age, or about the same age.

c. Marry a woman of the same or lower social class.

d. Marry a woman of a different complexion, lest children be too pale or too dark.

e. Marry a woman of a different height, lest children be too tall or too short.

f. If possible, avoid marriage to a widow or divorcée.

g. Don't marry for money.

Still, for all their rationality, the rabbis occasionally show sensitivity to physical beauty. For, after listing their detailed guidelines, they then say: "A woman who has beautiful eyes needs no further recommendation."

By the end of the talmudic period, Jewish marriage had truly begun to reflect both a religious and legal character. The customs and symbols of the modern wedding had emerged.

The Institution of the Shadchan

According to Jewish tradition, the successful matching of men and women in marriage is a responsibility requiring the wisdom of God. One legend holds that forty days before a child is born his or her mate is selected in heaven. The Talmud teaches that "God pairs two people even if He must bring them from one end of the world to the other." And rabbinic literature relates many instances of self-styled matchmakers who failed miserably because they doubted the difficulty of the task. Even so, the *shadchan*, the professional matchmaker, was for many centuries one of the most colorful Jewish figures.

1. Who was the first human matchmaker?

While Jewish tradition regards God as the supreme *shadchan*, the institution of matchmaking began in biblical times. In the Torah, the first *shadchan* we read about is Eliezer, servant of Abraham, who arranged the marriage of Isaac and Rebekah. It was not until the early Middle Ages, however, that matchmaking became a true profession.

2. What did the shadchan do?

The *shadchan* sought to arrange marriages that would please the parents of both the prospective bride and groom. As early as possible in the children's lives, the *shadchan* would approach both sets of parents with what seemed to him/her to be a "perfect match." The major goal for a match was compatibility; love was viewed as a secondary consideration. A good match, it was assumed, would help to engender love sometime later in life. During the late eighteenth and nineteenth centuries, love became a major reason for marriage among the Ashkenazim. This shift in attitude spelled the decline of the Ashkenazic *shadchan*. To this day, however, many Sephardic communities continue the practice of arranging marriages. Therefore, the *shadchan* is still with us.

3. What constituted a good match?

An ideal match, or *shidduch*, reflected some of the conditions we have discussed: similar social class, different complexion, different height, same approximate age, and so on. The *shadchan* looked for boys and girls who possessed good character and a high degree of piety. Above all, the *shadchan* tried to match scholarship to wealth, the rabbi's son, let's say, to the daughter of a learned, wealthy merchant.

4. Why scholarship and wealth?

During the era of the *shadchan*, the scholar held the highest position of status in the community. Brilliant students of Talmud commanded respect and honor from every Jew. Such a student was a real "catch." At the same time, wealth, then as now, made life more comfortable. A woman who could bring wealth into the home assured the scholar of untroubled study and the possibility of many children; wealth guaranteed the entire family a measure of security. In addition, from the *shadchan's* perspective, such a *shidduch* meant a higher fee, since that fee was calculated as a percentage of the dowry.

5. How was a shidduch formalized?

Once the *shadchan* had proposed a match and elicited a tentative expression of interest from both sets of parents, all parties involved engaged in preliminary negotiations. Among the items discussed were the size of the dowry (the money and possessions that the bride would bring to the marriage), which set of parents would provide which household furnishings, and the date and place of the wedding. Also negotiated was the *mohar* or bride price, the value in money or services that the groom would pay to the bride's father for the privilege of marrying his daughter. In Eastern Europe it was customary for the bride's parents to pledge full board (*kest*) for the groom in their home, generally for one year, so that he might pursue his talmudic studies without the need to go out and earn a living. Also included was a provision for penalty fees should one side or the other fail to fulfill its promises, and, of course, the *shadchan's* fee.

When everyone was agreed upon all the conditions and stipulations, a document known as the *tenaim* was written.

6. What was the document of the tenaim?

The *tenaim* (literally, "conditions") date to the third century C.E., when betrothal became a legal act. The *tenaim* were preliminary to the actual betrothal. Once signed, they were as binding as a marriage contract, requiring divorce for abrogation. In ancient times, signing of the *tenaim* took place one year prior to the actual wedding ceremony.

Beginning in the twelfth century, when betrothal and marriage were joined, the signing of the *tenaim* was advanced to just before the wedding. The *tenaim*, having been negotiated in advance, were read aloud and signed in the presence of two witnesses. In a practice known as *kinyan* (acquisition), the groom was asked if he was prepared to accept the *tenaim*. To acknowledge his agreement, he grasped a handkerchief extended by the rabbi in the presence of the two witnesses, who would later sign his marriage contract. A china dish was then broken by the two mothers of the bride and groom as a reminder of the destruction of the Temple and also, undoubtedly, to ward off evil spirits. With the couple now formally engaged, everyone present shouted *"Mazal tov!"* and partook of refreshments.

Reform Jews rarely sign *tenaim* today, but the practice is followed among many Orthodox and Conservative families before the wedding begins.

7. Did the shadchan arrange marriages for poor couples as well as wealthy ones?

Yes. While the financial remuneration was small in such instances, the *shadchan* considered matchmaking a *mitzvah* as well as a profession. Mindful of the rabbinic teaching that "he who has no wife is not a proper man," the *shadchan* sought to guarantee that every Jew in the community would have a spouse.

The Talmud teaches that one can sell a Torah to pay for a bride's dowry, so great is the value placed on the institution of marriage. Accordingly, a poor woman's dowry would often be provided by the community. A single Jew, or group of Jews, would make anonymous contributions to a special fund to avoid embarrassment of the bride. This was yet another demonstration of the value that Judaism attaches to the dignity of every individual.

The *shadchan*, work completed, could now look forward to the joyous wedding day, a day with many arrangements yet to be made.

Preparations for the Wedding in Times Gone By

Long before the bride and groom actually stood under the *chupah* to exchange their marriage vows, preparations for the ceremony were set into motion, preparations which were often extremely delicate and complex.

1. When could a Jewish wedding take place?

In times past, simply setting the date for a Jewish wedding was a challenge! First of all, there were (and are for traditional Jews) certain times of the year when marriage ceremonies were forbidden. These include: Shabbat; the festivals; fast days; the forty-nine days between the second night of Pesach and Shavuot, with the exception of Lag Ba'omer, the thirty-third day; the intermediate days of Pesach and Sukot; the period between two somber fast days during summer months, the 17th of Tamuz and the 9th of Av (Tishah Be'av).

After eliminating these dates, the couple then sought to schedule the ceremony on a day considered "lucky" in the context of their era and country. For example, German Jews liked to marry under a full moon, Spanish Jews under the new moon. Many Jewish communities favored a wedding during the first half of the month when the moon increases in size, seeing it as an omen of fortune, luck, and fertility.

Certain days of the week were considered particularly auspicious for marriages. Fridays were special favorites, inasmuch as they fell close to Shabbat, when having sexual relations with one's spouse was considered a double *mitzvah*. Virgins were most often wed on Friday, ideally immediately after Tishah Be'av, Shavuot, or Yom Kippur. Tuesdays and Thursdays were commonly wedding days for widows or divorcées, while Mondays and Wednesdays generally came to be regarded as unlucky times, though the Talmud mentions Sundays and Wednesdays as good wedding days for virgins. Some modern Orthodox Jews opt to marry on Tuesday, since it corresponds to the biblical day of creation, which God twice "pronounces" to be good.

2. Where was the ceremony held?

Ashkenazic and Sephardic Jews differed in their favored sites for weddings. The Ashkenazim held weddings outdoors, primarily as an expression of hope that, even as the descendants of Abraham were to be as numerous as the stars of the heavens (Genesis 22:17), so the union would be blessed with many children. An outdoor setting also mitigated against public displays of less than dignified behavior. Sephardic Jews, on the other hand, usually held their weddings indoors, most often in the synagogue. North American Jewry generally follows Sephardic practice, while modern Israeli weddings tend to be held outside.

3. What sort of clothing did the bride and groom have to purchase for the ceremony?

Jewish tradition teaches that all past sins of a bride and groom are forgiven as they begin their new life together. Accordingly, both the bride and the groom historically wore white as a symbol of purity. The bride's garb was a white dress, while the groom wore a *kittel* (a sort of white robe). This *kittel* was also often the garment in which the groom would be buried and therefore symbolized, not only purity and joy, but mortality as well.

In ancient Greece, in addition to white garments, both bride and groom wore garlands and wreaths. To this day some Sephardic couples don wreaths of bitter olive leaves as a reminder of the destruction of the Temple in Jerusalem, while some brides wear garlands of fragrant myrtle. In addition, both Sephardic and Ashkenazic grooms often wear a *talit*, a wedding gift from the bride or her parents.

4. Do the bride and groom exchange other gifts prior to the ceremony?

Yes. In times past, the groom gave the bride gifts such as a *siddur*, a wedding veil, fine combs, and a gold engagement ring. In addition to the *talit*, the bride often gave the groom gold or silver chains, a *haggadah*, and a beautiful watch. This custom of gift giving continues to the present time.

5. What was the minimum "guest list" for Jewish weddings?

Beginning in talmudic times, the rabbis required at least a *minyan* of ten male Jews, two of whom served as "witnesses." In Reform Judaism, a *minyan* is desirable but not required. Naturally, Reform counts women and men equally as members of the *minyan*.

6. What is an aufruf?

Aufruf (pronounced "owf-roof," or more colloquially "oof-roof") is a German word meaning "calling up" and refers to a synagogue celebration on the Shabbat preceding the wedding. The custom is biblically based. According to the Talmud, King Solomon built a gate in the Jerusalem Temple, where Jews would sit on Shabbat and honor

new grooms. When the Temple was destroyed in 70 C.E. and the institution of the synagogue gained strength, a form of the ancient Solomonic practice moved into the synagogue. Eventually, this custom became known as the *aufruf*.

7. What happens during an aufruf?

While few Reform temples currently observe the *aufruf*, it is a colorful part of many Conservative and Orthodox synagogues. On the Shabbat morning prior to the wedding, the groom is called to the Torah for an *aliyah* (honor of reciting the blessings before and after the reading of a section of the Torah). After he completes the concluding *berachah*, the congregation showers him with raisins, nuts, and sometimes candy, indicative of their good wishes for a sweet and fulfilling marriage.

8. Why raisins and nuts?

The rabbis invested the groom's being showered with raisins and nuts, usually almonds, with great symbolic significance. They indicated that, just as almonds and raisins may be either sweet or bitter, so a marriage may be either sweet or bitter. Furthermore, the Hebrew word for nut, *egoz,* is traditionally assigned the same numerical equivalent as the Hebrew words *chet* (sin) and *tov* (good). By the same token, the quality of a relationship turns on the character of those who are a part of it.

While many Reform congregations eschew the *aufruf,* they do have a special blessing ceremony for both the bride and groom on the Friday night or Saturday morning preceding the wedding.

The day of the wedding finally arrived. The bride had visited the *mikveh* (ritual bath), and many families had provided a feast for the community's paupers a day or two before, thus fulfilling the *mitzvot* of *tzedakah* and hospitality. The awesome moment approached. It was time for the wedding to begin.

9. What happened on the wedding day in times past?

The bride and groom awoke in their respective parents' homes and began a fast that ended only after the ceremony. As we have already seen, Jewish tradition teaches that all past sins are forgiven on a wedding day. Therefore, the day gradually acquired the characteristics of a quasi-Yom Kippur. Not only did the bride and groom refrain from food and drink, but they also recited the *viddui* (confession) of Yom Kippur in the afternoon service. Customarily, the wedding took place in the late afternoon, so as to enable as complete a fast as possible.

The rabbis of the Talmud saw the fast as a sign of contrition and, as importantly, as a guarantee of sobriety. They also perceived the fast as a reenactment of the drama of Sinai, where Israel, by accepting the Torah, consummated a "marriage" with God. Just as the Israelites fasted in preparation for their betrothal, said the rabbis, so it is fitting that a bride and groom do likewise. The custom of fasting is preserved by many Orthodox and Conservative couples today.

In Yemenite homes, even today, many grooms go to their mothers on their wedding day, asking her forgiveness for hurting her in the past. The son kneels and kisses her knees, after which his mother gives him a coin to be used as a ring substitute in the wedding service.

Yemenite wedding.

The Chupah and the Ring

"God creates new worlds constantly—by causing marriages to take place."

The Zohar

1. What about the chupah?

The use of the *chupah*, or marriage canopy, is a ritualization of the ancient rite of *nissuin*. As we have previously discussed, *nissuin* originally consisted of the wife being escorted to her husband's house to consummate the marriage. Over time, the *chupah* came to refer to a special room where the couple retired after the wedding service for a period of seclusion, known as *yichud*.

By the Middle Ages, the *chupah* had evolved into a canopy—symbolizing the home. This canopy was supported by four poles, under which the bride, groom, and family stood during the wedding.

Beginning in ancient times, when a boy was born, a cedar tree was planted. At the birth of a girl, an acacia tree was planted. When the children grew up, and were to be married, the poles with which to support their *chupah* were made from those very trees. Today, especially in Israel where cedar and acacia trees are plentiful, this ancient custom is preserved.

However, such elaborate preparations were not required. The *chupah* often was, and is, a plain *talit* or velvet cloth supported by four poles held by friends. In addition, the groom's *talit* was, and is, sometimes drawn over the heads of both him and his bride. In France, the groom covered the bride's head with his *talit* as a symbol of sheltering her. Modern Jews may use a *talit*, a free standing canopy, or some other portable *chupah* provided by the rabbi or synagogue.

2. Who bought the ring?

According to Jewish law, the groom was responsible for obtaining the ring. It could be a family heirloom or new, but it had to be the groom's property, inasmuch as he was giving it as a gift to the bride. Accordingly, the ring could not be borrowed.

3. Why a ring?

You will recall that one of the ways in which Jews became betrothed was through exchanging an object of value, usually a coin worth at least a *perutah* (roughly a penny). Over the centuries, this practice evolved into the custom of exchanging rings. Originally, only the bride received a ring. Today, of course, double ring ceremonies are quite common.

Both ancient and modern commentators have tried to explain the choice of rings as opposed to some other object. Some say that Jewish history is a chain of interlocking rings, and therefore the wedding ring symbolizes our link to the past and commitment to the future. Others look at the ring as a circle, having no beginning and no end. Similarly, they say, love never ends.

The Bible reflects a view of rings as a repository of power for good or evil. Pharaoh gives Joseph his ring and Joseph uses its authority to save Egypt. Ahashuerus, on the other hand, gives his ring to Haman, almost resulting in the destruction of the Jewish community. In like fashion, say some modern commentators, a husband and wife confer a certain power upon one another through exchanging rings, a power that must be used wisely, lest it damage the relationship.

4. What kind of rings did people use?

The rabbis insisted that the wedding ring be a metal band, lest there be any suspicion that the bride was marrying for the sake of a gift or lest the poor be embarrassed by their inability to "compete" with the rings of the wealthy. The ring was also to be without precious stones, so that the bride should not be misled as to its value.

5. Must you use a ring?

No. To this day, Sephardic Jews use a coin rather than a ring, usually the coin which mothers give their sons after the ritual of asking for forgiveness. In addition, more than one Jewish coin collector has used an actual *perutah* from antiquity as part of the wedding service in addition to the rings. This is a beautiful possibility, one which symbolically can bind us to our ancestors.

The bride and groom fasted. The *chupah* was erected. The wedding ring or coin was set aside in readiness. But no one forgot that marriage is a significant legal act. In addition to a joyous *simchah*, it is a serious agreement, a contract. Before the wedding ceremony, then, the contract had to be signed.

The Ketubah

1. What is the meaning of ketubah?

Ketubah literally means "written" and refers to the marriage contract signed and read at all Orthodox and Conservative weddings, and at a growing number of Reform ceremonies.

2. When did the ketubah originate?

Most scholars assert that the *ketubah* first emerged during the Babylonian exile, following the destruction of the Temple in 586 B.C.E. The Talmud, however, states that King David gave a *ketubah* to his wives, and Maimonides also assigns it an earlier date. Whenever it first came into use, the text was set about 200 B.C.E. and was composed in Aramaic, the Jewish community's most common language at that time.

3. What was the purpose of the ketubah?

Every bride received a *ketubah* from her groom, a legal document which protected her rights. The contract specified the groom's financial obligations, including a minimum divorce settlement and a minimum inheritance in case of the husband's death. In addition, the *ketubah* specified the Torah-based woman's right to food, clothing, and conjugal rights as well as the husband's responsibility to "care for her, provide for her, and cherish her." The Talmud elaborates on these basic Torah stipulations. Indeed, two talmudic tractates, *Kiddushin* and *Ketubot*, deal with marriage laws. Among other things, the laws state that a husband must:

    a. Give his wife a *ketubah*.

    b. Ransom her if she is kidnapped.

    c. Support her out of his estate (in the case of divorce) until she remarries.

    d. Support any daughters out of his estate until they are married or reach their majority.

Sexual fidelity was the right and responsibility of both partners. Neither mate could deny the other sex. In fact, there are even laws that specify the frequency with which intercourse must take place, depending on the husband's job and health considerations.

The wife had to go with her husband wherever he asked her to live, with two exceptions. She could demand that they establish a home in Palestine and, once there, demand that they live in Jerusalem.

The ancient *ketubah* represented a major step forward in women's rights. In a world in which women were often viewed as chattel, Judaism affirmed that every bride was to be accorded dignity and security in the marriage relationship.

4. How did the first ketubot look?

The *ketubah* originally was one of the great artistic "breakthroughs" of Jewish tradition. Usually on parchment, written by hand, and often illuminated in brilliant color, it manifested an artistic expression often stifled because of Judaism's prohibition against creating "graven images."

Over the centuries, every country in which Jews lived had *ketubot*, often containing symbols and objects that characterized that nation's unique folk art. In Persia, for example, the *ketubah* frequently included the lion of Judah, the rising sun of the Persian empire, and ornate oriental carpets. North

African *ketubot* had many geometric shapes, while Italian marriage contracts almost always portrayed cherubs.

Since, unlike the Torah, there is no rigidly fixed format for a *ketubah*, artists were not limited to parchment or to special pens or ink. Magnificent paper-cut *ketubot* were created, and, in time, printed *ketubot* such as those often seen today. The art of the *ketubah*, then, fulfilled the principle of *hiddur mitzvah*, "adornment of a *mitzvah*." To-day, centuries later, we still view the work of our forebears with admiration and awe.

5. Are ketubot different today?

Yes, in many ways. First of all, we have the benefit of high quality and high speed printing techniques. Dozens of beautiful *ketubot*, some reproductions of original art, have thus been made available on a mass scale. Then, too, there has been a resurgence in use of hand-made *ketubot*. Fine Jewish artists throughout the world have begun to devote their talent to the creation of stunning marriage contracts.

More significant than the change in style, however, has been the change in substance of the *ketubah*. Sensitive to the male-oriented language of the ancient document and contemporary values, many modern texts are "equalized." That is to say that *both* bride and groom make the same commitments, one to the other.

In years past, while Reform couples sometimes chose to have a *ketubah*, most Reform weddings were commemorated by the signing of a marriage certificate. Today, however, in response to the express wishes of growing numbers of Reform Jews, the Reform Movement has published its own *ketubot*, modern in style and language, but true to the spirit of our heritage.

6. When is the ketubah signed?

In ancient times, as today, the *ketubah* was signed just prior to the wedding ceremony. Prepared far enough in advance to be ready for the wedding, it required two male witnesses, unrelated to each other, the bride, or groom. Today, especially in Reform congregations, both men and women are honored by being asked to certify the beginning of a new couple's life together. In addition, the bride and groom themselves often sign the document.

7. When is the ketubah read?

As we shall see, the *ketubah* is read under the *chupah* between the sections of the ceremony known as *erusin* and *nissuin*. We have already learned how these two ceremonies, once separated by twelve months, ultimately became one. In ancient times, either the groom or the rabbi read the *ketubah* aloud to the bride. Today, while the rabbi most often reads the *ketubah*, some couples read the *ketubah* to one another.

You may decide to have a *ketubah*, whether hand-made or printed, as part of your wedding. If so, consult with your rabbi or Jewish bookseller long before the wedding date. An original *ketubah* can take many weeks to prepare, and, by the way, can be expensive. Still, a personal *ketubah* is a lifelong Jewish momento of one of the happiest days of your life.

The Jewish Wedding: The Modern Ceremony, Part One

"When a soul descends from heaven, it contains both male and female elements. The male elements enter a baby boy, the female elements a baby girl. And, if they are worthy, God one day reunites them in marriage."

The Zohar

We come at last to the actual wedding ceremony as it has emerged over the last several centuries. While many specifics of the Orthodox wedding have been changed and reinterpreted within the Reform, Conservative, and Reconstructionist Movements, it will be helpful to begin with an outline of Orthodox practice of the eighteenth-nineteenth centuries so as to better understand the thrust and rationale of subsequent reforms.

Scholars of the period tell us that in Eastern Europe the groom came to the courtyard of the synagogue at dawn, accompanied by his family, the rabbi, and his friends. Musicians, called *klezmorim*, led the way, sometimes in a torch-like procession, and usually playing a violin, bass, and clarinet. Shortly thereafter, the *klezmorim* departed, met the bride, and led her and her family to the courtyard. There, she and her groom were showered with barley, and all the assembled guests cried out *"Peru urevu"* ("Be fruitful and multiply") three times.

1. Do ceremonies today ever have klezmer music?

Yes. Especially in recent years, there has been a resurgence of interest in *klezmer*, and today there are a number of *klezmer* bands made up of young Jewish musicians who seek to preserve the rich *klezmer* heritage.

2. Why was the couple showered with barley?

Barley was a symbol of fertility, hence an expression of the community's hope that the young couple would have many children. A number of scholars believe that the Christian custom of throwing rice at a bride and groom as they leave the church grew directly out of this Jewish practice.

3. Why did people call out "Be fruitful and multiply"?

As we have previously learned, *peru urevu* is the first of the Torah's 613 commandments. As such, say the rabbis, it highlights Judaism's esteem for a family with children and, thus, was most appropriate as a good wish for the beginning of the wedding day.

4. What happened next?

The bride and groom went into separate rooms. In one room, the groom and the other males signed the *tenaim* (conditions) and prepared and signed the *ketubah* (marriage contract). Then the men surrounded the groom and danced with him. Meanwhile, the bride and her female entourage prepared for the customs of *bazetzen di kalah* ("seating of the bride") and *badeken di kalah* ("veiling of the bride").

5. What was bazetzen di kalah?

In the second room, the bride was seated on a beautiful, throne-like chair with her friends all around her. The chair was often covered with a white sheet and flowers. The *klezmorim* entered and cut off all of the bride's hair, replacing it with a *sheitl*, or wig. Afterwards, a singer called the *badchan* (jester) serenaded the bride with gloomy songs, allowing all present to give full expression to their feelings of nostalgia and sadness over the remarkable speed with which a child becomes an adult.

6. Why did the bride have her head shaved?

The Jews of Eastern Europe saw a woman's hair as a potentially powerful sexual temptation for men. Accordingly, a woman's locks were shorn and replaced with a wig, presumably to decrease her sexual appeal. While some ultra-Orthodox Jews still follow this practice, it has been all but totally eliminated in most branches of Judaism.

7. What about badeken di kalah?

Badeken di kalah, or "veiling of the bride," was the next formalized step on the path to the *chupah.* The groom entered and looked at the bride. Then he covered her face with the veil, while the biblical blessing over the matriarch Rebekah was recited: "Our sister, may you be the mother of . . . tens of thousands" (Genesis 24:60). The groom departed, after which the bride's friends danced around her, gently showering her with raisins and nuts.

8. Why do brides wear a veil?

The practice of wearing a veil derives from the account in Genesis 24:65 of how Rebekah covered her face with a veil when she saw her husband-to-be Isaac approaching. Over the centuries, other commentators saw the veil as a protection from the "evil eye," as a safeguard against lustful leering

by other men, and even as a means of insuring that the groom would not notice a pimple or scar on the bride's face and call off the wedding!

One beautiful interpretation asserts that, just as one often covers one's eyes during the *Shema* as an expression of concentration upon and trust in God, so does a bride cover her eyes as a symbol of trust in her husband.

9. Why did the groom personally veil his bride prior to the ceremony?

The Book of Genesis records the beautiful story of Jacob's love for Rachel. Jacob worked for Rachel's father Laban for seven years in order to win Rachel's hand in marriage. But,at their wedding, Laban secretly substituted his elder daughter Leah for Rachel, later asserting that Jacob had to marry her before marrying Rachel. As a result of that undoubtedly traumatic experience, Jewish grooms to this day assure themselves *before* uttering their vows that the woman they are marrying is in fact their intended.

10. What happened after badeken di kalah?

Immediately after *badeken di kalah,* the processional to the *chupah* began. First the *klezmorim* led the groom to the *chupah,* accompanied by his parents or by his father and father-in-law. Then they returned for the bride and her escorts, her parents, or her mother and mother-in-law. These escorts, or *shoshvinim,* carried candles and were often likened to a royal entourage, inasmuch as a bride and groom on their wedding day are truly like a king and queen.

11. When did the custom of shoshvinim originate?

The rabbis tell us that the angels Michael and Gabriel escorted Adam to his marriage to Eve. Thus, say the rabbis, the practice is biblical in origin, though it was formalized only in talmudic times.

12. Why did the escorts carry candles?

In Judaism, the marriage of a man and woman is likened to the joining of God and Israel in Sinai. The Book of Exodus 19:16 states that on the day the Torah was given "there was thunder and lightning" (i.e. lights). Just as there were lights at the bonding of God and Israel, so there are candles at a Jewish wedding.

It is fascinating to note that the Hebrew word for candle, *ner,* has a numerical equivalent of 250 and the sum of two candles equals 500. Further, the Hebrew phrase, *peru urevu,* "be fruitful and multiply," also has a numerical equivalent of 500!

In more recent times, the escorts were joined in some instances by married couples other than parents, called *unterfuhrers.* Together with the mothers and fathers, they brought the groom— dressed in his new *talit* and his *kittel*—and the bride—wearing her wedding gown—to the *chupah.* It was time to begin the ceremony.

The Jewish Wedding: The Modern Ceremony, Part Two

"On his wedding day, for every groom his bride is the most beautiful woman in the world."

The Talmud

With all the guests assembled, usually at least a *minyan* of ten, the wedding ceremony begins. The traditional order of the service is as follows:

1. The groom enters first and stands under the chupah.

Some interpreters state that, just as God waited at Sinai for His bride (Israel), so does the groom wait for his bride to appear.

2. The bride arrives at the chupah with her escorts, the shoshvinim and/or unterfuhrers.

In more recent times, this custom has been altered, with the father of the bride escorting his daughter down the aisle. The groom then walks to the father, shakes his hand, takes his bride's arm, and leads her to the *chupah*.

This practice may have its origin in the way some primitive societies arranged marriages. A father would lead his daughter between two lines of unmarried tribal males. Whoever reached out and "claimed" her had thus selected a wife. A father's escorting his daughter, then, is a "borrowed" rather than a uniquely Jewish custom.

3. The couple comes to the chupah, with the bride to the right of the groom.

The Book of Psalms 45:10 reads: "The queen stands on your right hand in gold of Ophir." Since a bride on her wedding day is seen as a queen, she stands on the groom's right.

4. The rabbi reads or chants a section from Psalm 118 and/or Psalm 100, then recites a medieval hymn.

Psalm 118:26 contains a traditional Jewish blessing of welcome: "Blessed are you who come in the name of the Lord." Psalm 100 is a psalm of thanksgiving, expressing thanks to and praise for God. The words of the medieval hymn are: "May the One who is mighty and blessed above all bless the groom and the bride."

5. The bride, with an entourage, circles the groom three or seven times.

While this custom is usually omitted from Reform ceremonies, it is a part of many Conservative and all Orthodox weddings.

The practice is based on a messianic verse from Jeremiah (31:22): "A woman shall court a man." The rabbis interpreted this sentence to indicate that a woman should "go around" a man, hence the custom of circling.

The more usual seven circles custom has been explained in a variety of ways:
  a. There are seven days in a week.
  b. There are seven *aliyot* on Shabbat.
  c. In the Bible it says "when a man takes a wife" seven times.
  d. There is a mystical teaching that the bride, in circling seven times, enters seven spheres of her husband's innermost being.
  e. On Simchat Torah, the Torahs are carried around the synagogue seven times.

Explanations for the basis of circling three times include:
  a. The three times in Hosea 2:21–22 when God, in reassuring Israel, "says": "and I will betroth you unto Me."
  b. A woman's three basic rights in marriage: food, clothing, sex.

Whether three or seven times, however, circling most probably reflected the structure of the family in times past. The custom implicitly made a statement that the bride's life revolved around her husband. The bride's circling also grew out of a mystical belief that, by making a ring around the groom, the woman thereby protected him from evil spirits.

Reform Judaism moved away from circling, in part because of the practice's superstitious overtones and in part because of Reform's insistence on the equality of the sexes. Still, the custom of circling remains a fascinating component of the Jewish wedding that some Reform couples choose to include.

6. The rabbi or cantor reads or chants the Betrothal Blessing.

We have already learned how two ceremonies, *kiddushin/erusin* and *nissuin*, originally separated by a one-year waiting period, were combined into a single rite in about the twelfth century. This next section of the service constitutes the *kiddushin/erusin* segment.

Kiddushin/erusin begins with a blessing over wine. The *Birkat Erusin* (Betrothal Blessing) is then recited or chanted. The bride and groom drink from the same cup, symbolically affirming that throughout life they will experience both joy and sorrow, but always together.

7. The groom places the bride's ring on her right index finger.

We recall that the three ancient modes of marrying included the giving and acceptance of an object of value, the giving and acceptance of a legal document, and cohabitation. The ring ceremony is symbolic of the first way. Traditionally, the ring is placed on the index finger of the bride's right hand, because it is the most prominent and so that the two required witnesses can see the ring easily.

Following the ceremony, the ring is moved to the more familiar third finger of the bride's left hand. This custom originated in about the fifteenth century and grew out of a belief that a vein in this finger runs directly to the heart. In many Reform ceremonies, the ring is placed directly on the third finger of the left hand.

8. The groom recites the legal formula of betrothal.

In the presence of the two witnesses the groom says: *Harei at mekudeshet li, betabaat zu, kedat Moshe ve'Yisrael.* "Behold you are consecrated unto me with this ring, according to the law of Moses and Israel."

In the Orthodox ritual, only the groom speaks, inasmuch as it is he who is "acquiring" a wife.

In the more liberal wings of Judaism, the bride will frequently respond with the same or a similar formula as she places a ring on the groom's hand.

With this single or joint recitation, the ceremony of betrothal concludes.

9. The ketubah is read.

The reading of the *ketubah* formally separates the betrothal and marriage ceremonies. As we have seen, it is a legal document, signed and witnessed prior to the ceremony, and calls to mind the second of the three ancient ways in which couples married.

The rabbi, a friend, or a group of friends may read the *ketubah* aloud, after which the groom hands it to the bride. It is thereafter her property.

Then, the marriage service (*nissuin*) begins.

The Jewish Wedding: The Modern Ceremony, Part Three

The marriage ceremony per se (*nissuin*) constitutes the consummation of the betrothal ritual (*kiddushin/erusin*) just completed.

1. A second cup of wine is filled.

According to Jewish law, one should not say the same blessing twice over the same cup of wine. Therefore, even though the *berachah* over wine is chanted or recited just minutes before, more traditional Jews will use a different cup for the *berachah* in the *nissuin* segment of the wedding ritual, which is, in fact, a separate ceremony.

2. The rabbi, cantor, or friends read or chant the Sheva Berachot.

The *Sheva Berachot* (literally, "Seven Blessings") are the heart of the marriage ceremony itself. The first *berachah* is the blessing over the wine, followed by blessings that praise God, extol the value of family life, and express hopes for the happiness of the bride and groom. The *Sheva*

Berachot are also sometimes called the *Birkat Nissuin.* After the blessings are completed, the bride and groom drink from the cup of wine.

Anyone may read or chant the *Sheva Berachot*, and many couples honor friends by asking them to participate in this way.

3. The groom breaks a glass.

The custom of breaking a glass at the conclusion of the wedding began in talmudic times. Many scholars assert that the most primitive origins of the practice reflected a symbolic breaking of the hymen. Over the centuries, however, various interpreters have held that the breaking of the glass:

  a. **Reminds us of the destruction of the Temples in Jerusalem.**
  b. Teaches that, in times of joy, we must always be cognizant that life also brings sadness and sorrow.
  c. Is, like marriage, permanent.
  d. Drove away satan and evil spirits, who, without this sudden noise, might have spoiled the occasion with some evil deed.
  e. Warns us that love, like glass, is fragile and must be protected.

Frequently, Reform and Conservative rabbis

will bless the couples just prior to the breaking of the glass with the traditional threefold benediction.

Many couples purchase a special glass to be broken in their ceremony. Increasingly, however, a light bulb rather than a glass is used. Jewish custom does not specifically prescribe a drinking glass, and a light bulb makes much more noise! The glass or bulb is wrapped tightly in a napkin before it is shattered. In some modern ceremonies, the bride as well as the groom breaks a glass.

4. Everyone yells "Mazal tov" or "Siman tov"!

"*Mazal tov*" and "*Siman tov*" are both Hebrew phrases which convey a sense of "congratulations." Ashkenazic Jews usually yell "*Mazal tov*," while Sephardim yell "*Siman tov*."

Interestingly, both phrases derive from astrology. *Mazal* literally means "planet"; *siman*, "omen." Thus, either exclamation amounts to wishing the new couple a "good horoscope" in addition to expressing a warm sentiment.

5. The couple spends a few moments alone before joining their friends and family.

This practice, called *yichud* or "privacy," is the traditional manner in which a man and wife symbolically recreate the third basic way in which couples married centuries ago. Today, traditional couples retire into a private room for a few minutes, break their wedding day fast, then emerge to join the celebration of this great occasion in

their lives. A formal period of *yichud* is not observed in most Reform ceremonies.

6. The celebration begins!

Extravagant wedding parties were never encouraged in Judaism. Indeed, a number of Jewish communities over the centuries (including modern Israel) actually passed legislation limiting their opulence. But, though Jewish custom frowns on ostentation, it is clear that a wedding banquet was and is cause for great joy and celebration, filled with music, dancing, and the fulfillment of the *mitzvah* to "make the bride and groom joyful."

Beginning in talmudic times, traditional Judaism asserted that a marriage should be celebrated for seven days, with the *Sheva Berachot* recited every day. Inasmuch as Jewish law requires a *minyan* in order to recite the blessings, the emphasis on a wedding as a major community event is clear.

7. Why seven days?

In the Book of Genesis 29:22, Laban prepares a feast for Jacob's wedding. After substituting Leah for Rachel, on the grounds that the eldest daughter had to be married first, Laban partially assuages Jacob's presumed anger by telling him: "Fulfill the *week* of this one, and we will give you the other also for the service, which you shall serve with me yet seven other years" (29:27). Laban's use of the word *week*, then, became the justification for the seven days of rejoicing.

Some commentators also point to Judges 14:12, in which Samson, having married Delilah, poses a riddle to his friends, challenging them to find a solution "within the seven days of the feast" (supposedly the feast celebrating his wedding).

8. Did you know?

a. Familiar modern wedding "personalities" such as flower girls, ring bearers, bridesmaids, and ushers do not derive from Jewish roots. They are all "borrowed" from other cultures.

b. The custom of the rabbi speaking at weddings did not begin until the Middle Ages.

·17·

THE JEWISH DIVORCE

Some Biblical History

Judaism exalts the beauty and sanctity of marriage and family life. No single traditional Jewish value is emphasized more than that of a man and woman joined together in matrimony and parenthood. Yet, thousands of years ago, our ancestors recognized and accepted the possibility that a relationship could fail, that two individuals could, for a variety of reasons, be unable to remain together. Accordingly, they made provision for the painful, yet sometimes necessary, act of divorce.

1. Who was the first couple to get divorced?

We don't know. But divorce clearly dates back to biblical times. The first recorded instance of a "separation" is that of Abraham and Hagar (Genesis 21). The Torah relates that Sarah was childless. Knowing that Abraham desperately wanted a child, she gave him her handmaid, Hagar, as a concubine, with whom he fathered a son, Ishmael. Once Isaac was born, however, Sarah demanded that Abraham send Hagar and Ishmael away. According to the Torah, Abraham did so, after God promised him that no harm would come to either mother or child. Ishmael subsequently became the father of the Arab nations, and, to this day, descendants of two sons of the same father are bitter enemies. Abraham did not technically marry Hagar, however, and thus we cannot single out this episode as a clear instance of divorce.

According to at least one modern interpreter, the first instance of a wife leaving a husband also involved Abraham, this time with Sarah. This inference is made on the basis of a careful examination of the Torah portion following the Akedah, the story of the "binding" of Isaac that we read on Rosh Hashanah. We recall the Torah account of God instructing Abraham to take Isaac to a mountain and prepare to sacrifice him. In the story, Abraham gets up early in the morning, takes Isaac, travels to Mount Moriah, and is about to act when an angel intervenes. At no time does the text refer to Abraham consulting *Sarah* in this matter!

The story of the Akedah ends, and Abraham returns home to Beer-sheba. This is immediately followed by an account of the death of Sarah. In spite of the fact that Abraham is wealthy and owns much land, Genesis tells us that Abraham has to *travel to another place*, Hebron, to mourn for Sarah, to weep for her, and to buy her a burial plot. Why?

Rashi suggests that Sarah died of sorrow and shock upon hearing what Abraham had done. Consequently, he had to journey from Mount Moriah to home to arrange for Sarah's funeral—in the same cave, by the way, in which legend holds that Adam and Eve are buried. The Ramban finds the passage problematic and tries to resolve it in a series of complex scenarios.

But a reading of Torah through twentieth-cen-

92·

tury eyes might suggest that Sarah's fury at the incident of the Akedah led her to *leave* her husband! Though not technically a divorce, it certainly is a fascinating interpretation.

2. When is divorce first mentioned in the Torah?

Deuteronomy makes clear reference to the existence of well-established divorce procedures among the Israelites: "When a man takes a wife and marries her, then it comes to pass that she finds no favor in his eyes because he has found some unseemly thing in her, that he writes her a bill of divorce, and gives it in her hand and sends her out of his house. . ." (24:1).

Though no specific divorcing couple is named in the Torah, it is clear that the practice existed and that the Israelites had developed a legal means of handling this difficult situation.

3. Does any couple get divorced in the Bible?

Yes. The prophetic Book of Hosea is, at least on the surface, the story of a divorce and subsequent reconciliation between husband and wife. Hosea marries a woman named Gomer. Gomer is a harlot and, in Chapter 2, Verse 4, Hosea sends her away with these words: "She is not my wife, and I am not her husband."

Again, we have a problem. Hosea severs his relationship with Gomer solely through an oral declaration, with no accompanying ritual. Furthermore, most commentators see this book as an allegory rather than as a historical account. Israel is the unfaithful wife, betrothed to God, yet pursuing other deities. God casts Israel out. Yet, in time, even as Hosea forgives Gomer, God takes Israel back as God's special people. We cannot, therefore, say that even this account exemplifies Jewish divorce as we have come to know it.

It is only with the writing of the Mishnah that Jewish divorce procedures are specified and cast in a carefully constructed legal context.

Divorce in the Talmud

By the time of the Mishnah, Jewish divorce law had been codified and specified in great detail. With the completion of the Talmud, the Mishnah plus the Gemara, the process of Jewish divorce was deemed important enough to require an entire tractate, called *Gittin*, dealing primarily with the dissolution of marriage. Marriage was now far more than a ritual. It was viewed as a legal contract. Accordingly, the termination of that contract through divorce demanded legal procedures.

1. What is the Hebrew word for divorce?

The Torah refers to a *Sefer Keritot* (literally, "Book of Cutting Off") as the document required for divorce. By rabbinic times, however, the terminology had changed. Jewish law, beginning in this period, called instead for a legal instrument known as a *get*.

2. What is the meaning of get?

Get is a Hebrew word meaning "certificate," with the added connotation of a document that terminates a relationship. Some scholars feel that the word "ghetto" derives from *get*, inasmuch as a ghetto separates one group of people from the rest of the community.

Get has a numerical equivalent of twelve (*gimel* = 3, *tet* = 9). When a *get* is written, it contains twelve lines of Aramaic text, detailing the particulars of the divorce, as we shall see. Beginning in the Mishnah, traditional Jewish law required the giving of a *get* when any marriage between two Jews ended, whether or not a religious wedding ceremony had taken place.

3. Who could initiate divorce proceedings?

Technically speaking, Jewish law provides only for a divorce action initiated by a husband, for it is always the husband who "gives" the *get*. In practice, however, the *bet din* (Jewish court) on occasion forced a husband to give his wife a divorce under certain circumstances.

4. What were considered sufficient grounds for a husband to divorce his wife?

A classic debate between the schools of Hillel

and Shammai dealt with just this issue. Shammai held that adultery was the only valid grounds for divorce, while Hillel affirmed that any reason was sufficient, even if a wife ruined a dish she was cooking. Rabbi Akiba went even further, stating that divorce should be permitted even if a man fell in love with a more beautiful woman.

Jewish law followed the school of Hillel in Mishnah times, the result being the right of a husband to divorce his wife "at will."

5. Didn't this legal ruling totally trivialize the Jewish value of marriage and family life?

On the face of it, yes. But a closer examination of these teachings reveals a profound sensitivity to the reality of the marriage bond. True, the Talmud states that a man may divorce his wife, even if she burned the soup. But Rashi's commentary on the text puts the letter of the law into perspective. When burning soup becomes a reason for divorce, says Rashi, the marriage could not have survived in any event.

There is a fundamental difference between marriage today and marriage in former times. Today, an aura of romantic love surrounds marriage. We are taught from early childhood that "love conquers all." It is easy to get married and hard to get divorced.

Historically, Judaism's perspective was different. Parents arranged marriages. Romantic love was not necessarily a factor. Financial security and a compatible family background were the primary considerations. Contracts assured that every contingency was covered. Jewish law required a lengthy engagement. "Dating" was unheard of. In short, it was hard to get married. Accordingly, early Jewish law's liberal divorce provisions seem to indicate an attitude that, if all prior preparations did not result in a good relationship, it was better to end it rather than prolong unhappiness and anguish.

6. Why was the wife powerless in the case of divorce?

During the time of the Mishnah, Jewish law spoke of a man "acquiring" a wife, almost as one acquired property. During the eleventh century, however, Rabbenu Gershom ruled that a wife had to agree to the divorce, except in the case of adultery. The husband still "gave" the get, but by mutual consent.

7. Surely Jewish law gave some more specific guidelines on grounds of divorce?

Yes. The law provides that a man may divorce his wife under the following circumstances, to name a few: (1) if she refuses him sex, (2) if she refuses to work in the house, (3) if she has no children after ten years of marriage, (4) if she commits adultery, (5) if she insults him or his father, (6) if she is morally indecent in public, (7) if she is lax in religious observance.

On the other hand, the bet din could force a husband to give his wife a divorce if: (1) he refused her sex, (2) he had boils, a goiter, or some other physical problem or disease that made him disgusting to her, (3) he gathered excrement or smelled badly as a result of his profession, (4) he was cruel to her, (5) he would not allow her to visit her parents, (6) he converted to another faith, (7) he acted immorally, (8) he was lax in religious observance, (9) he was impotent or sterile, (10) he refused her support—food, clothing, and shelter.

8. Was there any attempt to save a marriage in trouble?

Definitely. Every effort was made to keep a couple together before a divorce was granted, as we shall see.

The Jewish Divorce: The Rights and Responsibilities of Husband and Wife

We have already enumerated a number of grounds for Jewish divorce. A closer examination of them reveals that they were carefully developed and, in most instances, reflected important Jewish values as well as a deep respect for women's rights.

1. Why was denial of sex grounds for divorce?

In Judaism, unlike in some religions, sex is not regarded as evil or unseemly. Though procreation is a *mitzvah,* Judaism treats sex as a healthy reflection of tenderness and love between husband and wife. Accordingly, the refusal of sex mitigated against both the continuity of the Jewish people and a loving human relationship between the couple. Both partners were equally responsible.

A wife who refused her husband was liable for the loss of her *ketubah,* in addition to divorce. A husband who declined sex could be fined and ultimately forced to give his wife a divorce.

Women's rights in sexual matters were made explicit in the Talmud. Indeed, the minimum sexual obligations of a man were specified clearly. Husbands who did not work were expected to make love with their wives every day, laborers twice a week, donkey drivers once a week, camel drivers a minimum of once every thirty days, and sailors once every six months. This law also clearly had the effect of limiting how long a man could be away from home. However, men were enjoined not to force sex on their wives, with the warning that this would result in unworthy children.

2. How was the Jewish value of family sanctity reflected in the divorce laws?

It is interesting to note how many grounds for divorce in Jewish law relate to a reverence for the family. A Jewish wife could seek a court-ordered divorce if her husband refused to allow her to visit her parents, if he converted to another faith, if he was lax in religious observance, if he

insulted or was cruel to her, or if he physically abused her. In similar fashion, a husband, whose wife cursed his parents in his presence, who did not have children after ten years of marriage, who was lax in religious observance or morally indecent in public, was well within his rights to ask for a divorce. We see, then, that halachic expectations as to the nature of a marriage extended well beyond the man-woman relationship. They also included respect for parents and religious practice.

3. Was serious emotional illness grounds for divorce?

The giving of the *get* is a legal procedure. It therefore requires that those involved in the dissolution of the marriage contract be competent. An insane husband could not initiate a divorce proceeding, then, while an insane wife could not be divorced (except with the permission of 100 rabbis), inasmuch as she was not competent to accept the *get* of her own free will.

4. What if a husband disappears and never returns?

In modern law, a person missing for seven years is presumed dead. Jewish law, sadly, makes no such provision, resulting in the tragic status of the *agunah,* or "chained woman." Unless the body of her husband is actually recovered, or unless at least one witness attests to the death, the wife cannot ever remarry under Jewish law. She is considered married. Should she remarry civilly, the marriage has no religious status and the children are considered bastards. The instance of the *agunah,* though undoubtedly motivated by hope that a husband will return safely, today remains a painful challenge to modern Orthodoxy, especially in the State of Israel.

5. What are some additional grounds for divorce that are especially sensitive to women?

The Mishnah stipulates that a husband who refuses to allow his wife to work in the home must divorce her and pay her *ketubah.* Rabbi Simeon ben Gamaliel was especially emphatic on this point, asserting that forced idleness leads to madness.

Jewish law also allows for divorce when conditions are such that the wife simply finds the marriage untenable. If, for example, she freely married a man who had boils or who smelled badly and later decided she just could not stand him, the Mishnah permitted a divorce. In commenting on this unfortunate possibility, Maimonides stated: "If a woman says: 'My husband is repulsive to me, I cannot live with him,' the court forces the husband to divorce her, because a wife is not a prisoner."

6. What mechanisms existed for reconciliation before a divorce?

Jewish law made every effort to salvage a marriage, if at all possible. Nowhere is the view of divorce as a last resort more obvious than in the talmudic story of Rabbi Meir and the banished woman. According to the Talmud, a certain woman attended the regular weekly lectures of Rabbi Meir and, as a result, came home later than her husband wished. In anger, he banished her from the house and told her that she could not return until she spit in the rabbi's eye.

Rabbi Meir heard of the situation and, in public, asked the woman to spit in his eye, ostensibly to relieve pain. She did so, and her husband took her back. In short, a distinguished rabbi suffered public indignity in order to save a marriage.

But sometimes even the best efforts fail. Divorce becomes inevitable. And so we turn to the last resort, the ritual of the giving of the *get*.

The Get

"When love is strong, a man and woman can make their bed on a sword's blade. When love grows weak, a bed of sixty cubits is not large enough."

Talmud

"When a man divorces the wife of his youth, God's very altar weeps."

Talmud

1. Who requires a get?

According to Jewish law, a *get* (bill of divorce) is required for every Jewish marriage, whether or not there was a religious wedding ceremony. The sole exception is a marriage between a Jew and a non-Jew, which is not considered valid in the view of *halachah* and therefore requires no *get*. All Conservative and Orthodox rabbis require a *get* from any prior marriages as a precondition for officiating at a wedding. A *get* is also required in the State of Israel.

Reform Judaism as a Movement does not require a *get*, holding that civil divorce is sufficient. Still, many Reform rabbis strongly suggest a *get*, and at least one Reform rabbi has developed his own ceremony of Jewish divorce.

2. Why do many Reform couples today obtain a get?

Whatever one's personal feelings regarding the *get*, it may be that a future marriage will involve a Conservative, Orthodox, or Israeli partner. Then, too, life often takes us far away from a former spouse. Accordingly, many couples choose to complete the divorce ritual promptly in anticipation of future circumstances and as a matter of convenience.

There is another reason, however, which seems to motivate those participating in the divorce ritual. Judaism marks every significant occasion in the life cycle. At the time of a divorce, with all its trauma and pain, Jewish ritual forces acknowledgment of the reality of divorce while at the same time pointing to the future.

3. Who officiates at a Jewish divorce?

The ritual of the giving of a *get* is generally conducted by a *bet din* ("court") of three rabbis. Also in attendance are two witnesses selected by the *bet din*, a *sofer* or scribe who writes the *get*, and the husband and wife. Both husband and wife must be known to the witnesses, either personally or through carefully substantiated identification.

4. What does a get look like?

A *get* is a document of twelve lines, written in Hebrew and Aramaic in Torah script with a quill pen. The twelve lines correspond to the twelve lines of empty space separating the first four books of the Torah. As we have already seen, the Hebrew word *get* also has a numerical equivalent of twelve.

5. What information does a get contain?

There are five basic components to a *get*:
a. A statement that the husband divorces his wife without duress or compulsion.
b. A provision that after the *get* the husband and wife may have no further relationship.
c. The time and place of the writing of the *get*.
d. All of the husband's and wife's Hebrew and English names, plus their fathers' Hebrew and English names, plus their fathers' religious status (if a *kohen* or a Levite).
e. Composition on unattached, self-contained parchment.

6. How long is the ritual?

Approximately two hours, and by design. The length of the ceremony assures that the *get* will have no errors. As importantly, it originally provided the couple with time to carefully consider their decision, and possibly a chance of reconciliation.

7. What is the nature of the ceremony?

In a sense, the *get* ritual is the reverse of a wedding ceremony. In the eyes of Jewish law, the *get* also marks a woman's reacquisition of self, just as she was "acquired" in the wedding ceremony.

8. What is the order of the ceremony?

Today, outside of Israel, a civil divorce must generally be obtained in advance of the couple's appearances before the *bet din*. In Israel there is no Jewish civil divorce, only a religious one. All custody, property, and monetary decisions must also have been settled prior to the ceremony. Then the ritual begins:
a. The husband formally appoints the *sofer* to write the *get* and the witnesses to sign it.
b. The *bet din* questions the couple to assure their joint consent to the divorce and to ascertain all of the information to be included in the *get*.
c. The *sofer* writes the *get* in the presence of the husband, the witnesses, and the *bet din*.
d. The witnesses sign the *get*.
e. The husband or his representative actually places the *get* into the hands of the wife and declares his decision to divorce her.
f. The wife places the *get* under her arm and walks a few steps to symbolically acknowledge that it is her possession.
g. The husband leaves.
h. The *bet din* members cut the *get* crosswise so that it cannot be reused.
i. The wife leaves.

The original *get* is retained by the *bet din* as a permanent record. Both husband and wife receive a copy confirming the action shortly thereafter.

9. How soon after the get is given may the couple remarry?

According to Jewish law, the husband may remarry at once. The wife is required to wait at least ninety-two days so that the paternity of any possible pregnancy will not be in question. *Halachah* also holds that the wife cannot marry a *kohen*, since *kohanim* are proscribed from marrying a divorcée. Outside of these restrictions, however, both husband and wife are now free to seek out and find new happiness, new fulfillment, new love, hopefully with new wisdom as well.

·18·

DEATH AND MOURNING

The Moment of Death

"To everything there is a season, and a time to every purpose under heaven—a time to be born, and a time to die. . . ."

Ecclesiastes 3:1,2

The wise person understands that death is a part of life. Yet, because of the finality that death represents and the fear and anxiety that its mere contemplation produces, it is a subject that is all too often totally avoided. As a result, the death of a parent, spouse, relative, or friend often leaves us paralyzed, not only emotionally, but in terms of knowing what Judaism prescribes as a response to the passing of a loved one.

One Jewish thinker has asserted that the ultimate purpose of all religions, Judaism included, is to respond to our finitude, to the inevitability of our own death. If so, the psychological brilliance of Jewish wisdom and insight is nowhere more evident than in the manner in which it addresses death and mourning.

1. What is the Hebrew word for death?

The Hebrew word for death is *mavet*. Interestingly, the name of the ancient Canaanite god of the underworld was Mot, derived from the same linguistic root. Accordingly, some scholars feel that the term was borrowed, though it is unclear as to who borrowed the designation from whom.

2. What is the meaning of the Hebrew word goses?

The word *goses* is used to refer to a dying person. Once it is apparent that death is inevitable, the immediate family gathers at the home or hospital to share its strength in the face of impending pain.

3. What do we do ritually when the death of a loved one seems imminent?

Traditional Judaism delineates a highly ritualized procedure. Though Liberal Jews have modified these customs considerably, it is instructive to know what the customs are, their origins and rationale. Strict Orthodox practice includes:
   a. A "confession" (in Hebrew, *viddui*) or recitation of the *Shema* by the dying person.
   b. A constant presence in the room by members of the immediate family.

4. Why do some Jews change the name of a person who is critically ill?

This custom derives from a talmudic belief that it is possible to confuse the angel of death by changing a loved one's name, thereby causing it to move on in search of someone not present.

Men are often given the name Chaim while women are named Chayah, both meaning life. The ritual often brings a measure of psychological comfort to the family and is practiced by some Liberal as well as Orthodox Jews.

5. Does Judaism really have a ritual of confession?

Yes, but one totally unlike that of Christianity. In Catholicism, confession is a sacrament, offered in private to a priest who serves as an intermediary between the individual and God. In Judaism, confession of shortcomings most often occurs in a communal setting, on Yom Kippur in the synagogue. There is a collective expression of atonement for sins ("For the sin which *we* have sinned against You . . .") as well as atonement through personal prayer, but never through an intermediary. The Jew prays directly to God and, indeed, may ask forgiveness for sins at any time, in or out of the synagogue.

The traditional Jewish deathbed confessional consists of the following affirmation:

"I acknowledge before You, O Lord my God and God of my ancestors, that my life and death are in Your hands. May it be Your will to heal me. But, if death is my fate, then I accept it from Your hand with love. May my death atone for whatever sins I have committed before You. In Your mercy, grant me the goodness that awaits the righteous and bring me to eternal life.

Father of the orphans, Protector of the widows, guard my loved ones to whom my soul is joined. Into Your hands I return my spirit, for You will redeem me, eternally faithful God.

Shema Yisrael Adonai Elohenu Adonai Echad.

Hear, O Israel: the Lord is our God, the Lord is One."

The dying person often continues with a prayer from the Yom Kippur confessional as well. Today, though the *viddui* is still utilized, many Jews recite only the *Shema* in its place.

6. How did the Shema come to be a Jew's last affirmation?

No one knows for certain, but there is ample evidence that this custom was already well established by the rabbinic period. One midrash, for example, relates that, when Jacob (also known as Israel) was about to die, he gathered his children about him and asked them if they would commit themselves to the Covenant. According to the midrash, they replied with the *Shema*, both in its literal sense and with the meaning "Hear, O Israel [Jacob our father]: the Lord is [and shall be] our God, the Lord is One." When the great Rabbi Akiba was being tortured by the Romans, he is reported to have uttered the *Shema* with his dying breath, and countless Jewish martyrs throughout history followed this example, affirming their utmost faith in God, even at the moment of death.

7. Why does the family remain in the room at the moment of death?

This is an act of the highest respect and caring. Just as we do not come into the world alone, so we should not leave it alone. In the last moment of a person's life, he or she should, if possible, be surrounded by the family that was so much a part of his or her being. However, if being in the presence of a dying person presents the danger of a severe psychological trauma or of physical illness to any family member, that individual may and should leave the room.

8. Is there a prayer to recite at the moment of death?

Yes. When death comes, the eyes and mouth of the deceased should be closed and the body covered with a sheet. Then, those present may recite the following: *Dayan ha'emet,* "true Judge." A full *berachah* including these words is also recited prior to the funeral service, as we shall see. When our loved one is gone, Jewish law and custom specify a series of acts that have two aims:

a. Showing honor to the deceased (in Hebrew, *kevod hamet*).
b. Helping the living.

It is to this elaborate and intricate ritual and human support system that we now direct our attention.

Preparing the Body for Burial

Immediately following the death of a loved one, the shock and pain of loss can immobilize us. For many Jews, a call to the local Jewish funeral home relieves the family of the responsibility of caring for the body and making preparations for burial. We should be aware, however, that there is a highly structured series of procedures following death and prior to burial that is part of Orthodox Jewish practice. While a number of these practices are not generally observed by Liberal Jews, an examination of them can teach us a great deal about traditional Jewish values as they are acted out in time of tragedy.

We have already mentioned that the eyes and mouth of the deceased are closed at the moment of death. This is, of course, an act of respect to the departed. But, there were those who felt that this practice had an additional, mystical rationale. We close the eyes, they said, so that the person's ghost might not reenter the body, and the mouth so that the soul might not be tempted to tarry in this world. Accordingly, these Jews would also open the windows of the room so that the soul might escape. To the modern mind, beliefs and practices such as these may seem like sheer superstition. The fact is, however, that we have no greater certitude regarding what happens to us after death than did our ancestors of centuries past.

1. What is Orthodox practice following death?

Following the death of a loved one, Orthodox Jews may:

a. Observe the ritual of *keriah*.
b. Place the body face up with its feet toward the door.
c. Place candles at the head of the body.
d. Pour out all standing water in the room or home.
e. Cover all mirrors in the home.
f. Recite Psalm 91 and Job 1:21.
g. Call the *chevrah kaddisha* to prepare the body for burial.
h. Secure a *shomer* to remain with the body until the funeral.

2. What is keriah?

Keriah is a Hebrew word meaning "tearing" and refers to a ritual in which clothing or a black ribbon is cut or torn as a sign of mourning. Orthodox Jews formerly "cut *keriah*" at one of two times, either at the moment of death or at the time of the funeral. Today, all Jews generally cut *keriah* just prior to the funeral service.

3. What is the origin of keriah?

The custom derives from a number of biblical stories in which rending one's garments reflected grief and anguish:

a. Jacob, on hearing of Joseph's supposed death (Genesis 37:34).
b. David, when told of Saul's death in battle (II Samuel 1:11).
c. King David and his servants, in mourning for David's son Absalom (II Samuel 3:31).
d. Job, grieving for his children (Job 1:20).

Over time, the custom attained the force of law, a practice that replaced the mutilation of flesh practiced by many pagan peoples.

4. How do we cut keriah?

Only those in the immediate family of the deceased cut *keriah*. In Orthodoxy, only one's actual clothes may be used, a coat or dress. The tear in the garment is never repaired completely, symbolic of the permanent tear in our lives which the death of a loved one brings. Liberal Jews will often use a black ribbon provided by the funeral home in place of clothing.

Keriah is always performed standing, just as Job "stood up and rent his clothes" when his children died (Job 1:20).

A cut is made on the left side, closest to the heart, for parents and on the right side for all others. If *keriah* is performed at the moment of death, before the garment or ribbon is cut, the immediate family recites *Dayan ha'emet*.

If, as is now almost universal custom, *keriah* is performed prior to the funeral service, a full *berachah* is recited: *Baruch Atah Adonai Elohenu Melech ha'olam Dayan ha'emet*. "Blessed are You, O God, Ruler of the universe, the true Judge."

5. Why is the body placed face up with its feet toward the door?

No one knows for certain how this custom originated. Certainly the body was kept face up (and
covered with a sheet) to preserve the dignity of
the deceased. The positioning of the body probably
derives from a superstitious belief that the eyes
of the corpse must not be positioned to look back
into the home where he or she lived, lest his or
her ghost be tempted to reenter the home and
dwell among the living.

6. Why are candles lit at the head of the body?

When death is imminent, candles are often
lit in the room in which the *goses,* the "dying
person," lies. These candles, symbolic of the flick-
ering soul, are kept burning after death. Many
scholars say that this custom was originally designed to ward off evil spirits. In modern times,
it has been interpreted as the light of memory
which our loved ones leave with us as a perpetual
legacy.

7. Why is all standing water poured out?

Once again, we are struck at how superstition
led to the emergence of Jewish customs in the
face of death's mystery. There were many who
believed that the ghost of the deceased might
inhabit the house. Among these individuals, it
was commonly held that ghosts and spirits could
not cross water. Therefore, eliminating all standing water precluded the possibility that spirits
might be trapped in the house, unable to depart.

8. Why are all mirrors in the home covered im-mediately following death?

The custom of covering mirrors in a house of
mourning has had many interpretations. The practice undoubtedly originated out of a belief that
the mirror image of a dead body would portend
another death in the coming year, or that the
mirror could trap the soul of the deceased or another family member in some way. In modern
times, covering mirrors has been seen as a means
of freeing mourners from all thoughts of physical
beauty or attractiveness at a time of loss. Since
the Orthodox mourning process precludes shaving
or the use of makeup, as we shall see, we cover
the mirrors to remove all temptation to violate
these prescriptions.

9. Why especially is Psalm 91 recited?

In times of both personal and national disaster,
the words of comfort and faith that psalms express
have been a source of consolation and hope to
Jews for many centuries. At a time of loss, Psalm
91 was seen as especially appropriate since it speaks
of God taking us "under the shelter of His wings."
In all likelihood, the people themselves "chose"
this psalm by turning to it in grief. Their choice
became Jewish custom.

10. What is the chevrah kaddisha?

Chevrah kaddisha literally means "holy society"
and refers to a group of individuals within the
Jewish community whose chosen task is to prepare
the body for burial in strict accordance with Jewish
law.

Water scoop used by the chevrah kaddisha *to cleanse the body of the dead.*

The *chevrah kaddisha* originated several hundred
years ago, part of a communal system for assuring
what we in Reform Judaism today refer to as "the
caring community." There were *chevrahs*—or *cha-
vurot*—whose job it was to visit the sick, to provide
dowries for poor women so that they could be
married, and to perform a host of other caring
acts, by the people and for the people. The *chevrah
kaddisha* was one of those groups and remains so
today.

11. What does the chevrah kaddisha do?

The *chevrah kaddisha* cares for the body of the deceased from death until burial. Either in the house or in the funeral home, the members perform a series of highly ritualized acts known as *taharah*, "purification," of the corpse. In a strictly prescribed sequence, they wash the body and dry it while reciting prayers and psalms. During the entire procedure, the face of the departed is never down. In Jewish law, *taharah* is regarded as a great *mitzvah*, to be undertaken without compensation of any kind. It is an act of *chesed shel emet* (literally, "a loving deed of truth") without ulterior motive.

12. Where does the phrase chesed shel emet come from?

In the Book of Genesis (47:29), the patriarch Jacob realizes that he is about to die. He summons his son Joseph and asks him to see to his burial, to "deal kindly (*chesed*) and truly (*emet*) with me." Based on this touching story of father and son, seeing to the dignified burial of a loved one became even more of a precious duty.

13. What happens once the body is washed?

In Orthodoxy, the *chevrah kaddisha* dresses the body in a simple white shroud (in Hebrew, *tachrichim*). Beginning in the first or second century C.E., a ruling by the great Rabban Gamaliel established the principle that all Jews were equal in death and mitigated against ostentation in funer-

als. The handmade shroud symbolized, not only equality, but also purity and dignity. *Tachrichim*, then and now, have no pockets, expressing Jewish belief that our material possessions cannot accompany us beyond the grave. *Tachrichim* may be made of linen, cotton, or muslin and are uniformly white in color.

Reform Jews usually do not employ the services of a *chevrah kaddisha*, nor are the dead buried in shrouds. There are many varying customs, which we shall examine later.

14. What is the role of the shomer?

In Orthodoxy, a corpse is never left alone from the moment of death until burial, as a sign of respect to the departed. The *shomer* is a devout Jew who stays with the body until the funeral. In former times, the *shomer* guarded against rats and body snatchers and also ostensibly against evil spirits getting to the body. He also constantly recited psalms, a custom which continues to the present. The *shomer* is not a member of the *chevrah kaddisha* and is generally paid for his services. Reform Jews usually do not engage a *shomer*.

While we may or may not find all of these Orthodox practices edifying or meaningful, they embody a powerful message and an important Jewish value. In death, as in life, we care for our loved ones and take steps to ensure that their departure from this earth is dignified.

What Happens After We Die?

Jewish positions on a variety of issues relating to death and mourning derive in part from Jewish responses to the question: "What happens after we die?" Therefore, before addressing these subjects, we must first review a spectrum of Jewish views relating to life after death and the normative response that came to inform halachic rulings.

1. The biblical view.

In the Torah, and in the *Tanach* in general, there is virtually no intimation of a belief in a heaven or hell, or in physical resurrection. The Bible does mention a shadowy place called *Sheol*, but it is not described in great detail. It was conceived of as a pit beneath the earth, a place of darkness and quiet, separated from our world. The essential thrust of the biblical idea, however, is that the good will be rewarded and the evil punished in *this* life, rather than in some hereafter. Accordingly, it is clear that the Bible emphasizes our life here on earth, with no promise of a future physical existence of any kind.

2. In Second Temple times.

One of the most difficult problems that any religion must confront is the reality that the good do suffer and the evil do often prosper. Indeed, that is the dilemma posed by the Book of Job, whose only answer is that there is no way for human beings to understand "God's plan." The reality of life made the biblical notion of reward and punishment seem naive. Accordingly, about the fifth century B.C.E., a new notion began to gain credence in the Jewish community.

Jews embraced the idea of life after death and physical resurrection. There would come a day, said these Jews, when a Messiah would come and raise the dead. At that time, the Jews will be restored to the Land of Israel, where a descendant of the House of David will sit on the throne in a world of peace.

3. In the Talmud.

By talmudic times, the Pharisaic belief had been elaborated into a full-blown system of physical resurrection and immortality of the soul. The Messiah would bring *olam haba,* a perfect world.

4. A mystical answer.

During the Middle Ages, Jewish mystics outlined a belief in *gilgul hanefesh,* a transmigration of souls, or reincarnation. According to the mystics, every person has a soul and a task to accomplish here on earth. If the task is completed in the course of a lifetime, the soul ascends to God after death. If not, the soul returns to earth in a different vessel again and again—until its job is done. If the soul engages in great evil, it may be punished and wander eternally. This unending wandering was the greatest punishment that the mystics could conceive.

5. A rationalist answer.

The twelfth-century philosopher Maimonides was one of Judaism's most brilliant thinkers. Because of the highly controversial nature of his intellectual views, he wrote on two levels: for the "masses" and for other philosophers. The words he used were the same for both audiences but "equivocal" in nature. Only if you knew the "code" could you know the "truth."

On the face of his writings, Maimonides appeared to believe in physical resurrection. Indeed, his "Thirteen Articles of Faith" included physical resurrection as an essential tenet for every Jew.

A careful reading of Maimonides' work, however, reveals that he was a rationalist. For Maimonides, God is pure intelligence. Therefore, whatever immortality we humans achieve is through our intellect. The greater the thoughts we think, the closer we come to God's "thoughts" and thereby to immortality.

6. Reform Judaism's answer.

Reform Judaism rejected all notions of a single Messiah, of bodily resurrection, and of a physical life after death. Instead, Reform embraced a belief in the immortality of every soul, holding that all souls return to God.

A perfect world, said the Reformers, can come about only in a Messianic Age, a time when all people become co-partners with God in creating a heaven on earth. Further, our true immortality resides in the memories treasured in this world by those who knew and loved us.

One explicit message emerges from this brief overview of Jewish views of the afterlife. Regardless of the details of any position or any thinker, Judaism never compromised its insistence on the absolute necessity of a good and decent life in *this* world. The Talmud states: "Better is one hour of repentance and good works in this world than all the life of the world to come." So long as we keep that value clearly in mind, we can begin to address the rituals and practices that these philosophies produced over time.

Jewish Positions on Autopsy, Embalming, and Cremation

1. What is the Orthodox position on performing autopsies?

There is no law in the Bible, Talmud, or subsequent codes of *halachah* which expressly forbids autopsy. Indeed, it is clear from classic Jewish literature that autopsies were performed upon occasion and that the rabbis knew anatomy quite well. Still, an aversion to autopsy was a custom that gradually acquired the force of law.

There were essentially three reasons that led to the Orthodox stance. The first was an insistence on a speedy burial of the entire body. The body was to be intact, since physical resurrection was contemplated. Even limbs amputated during one's lifetime were to be placed in the coffin. Since an autopsy could result in a violation of this principle, it was discouraged.

A second factor was the Jewish value of *kevod hamet,* "respect for the dead." A corpse was regarded as holy and autopsy as a disgraceful handling of the body of a loved one.

A third major objection derived from the rabbinic ruling that we may not use the dead for the *supposed* benefit of the living. But because of this *conditional* wording, autopsy came to be permitted under certain conditions.

2. What were the conditions under which autopsy was condoned?

The great eighteenth-century Jewish scholar Rabbi Ezekiel Landau of Prague ruled that, if the knowledge gained through an autopsy could *clearly* save the lives of others in the community on a *near-term basis,* then it could be justified. An autopsy was forbidden if the sole purpose was to teach anatomy or on the *chance* that knowledge could be gained. It was a procedure countenanced only on the grounds of immediate life-saving benefit to that particular community.

3. How do Liberal Jews view autopsy?

Our ancestors could not have foreseen the age in which we live, a time in which the most minute piece of scientific evidence can be communicated instantly throughout the world. Accordingly, the findings of an autopsy performed in a small town in the United States have the capacity to save the lives of countless men and women throughout the world. Therefore, the majority of Jews have come to accept autopsy as an important scientific procedure, with many scholars citing an expanded interpretation of Rabbi Landau's ruling as a rationale for their endorsement. Strict Orthodox Jews, however, continue to reject autopsy, except in the most clear-cut circumstances.

4. What about embalming?

Orthodox practice prohibits embalming, which is a procedure that slows the process of bodily decomposition. It is interesting to note that the Torah mentions that both Jacob (Genesis 50:2–3) and Joseph (Genesis 50:26) were embalmed, but in accordance with *Egyptian* rather than Jewish custom.

Embalming is seen as *nivul hamet,* a "desecration of the body." Also, since embalming delays the decomposition of the body and since Orthodoxy views decomposition of the body as a necessary precondition for the ultimate atonement for sins, embalming is seen as a barrier to that atonement.

Finally, since blood is part of the body, embalming violates the Orthodox commitment to bury the body "intact" in order that it might be resurrected whole.

Reform Judaism has no official position on embalming, and therefore the dead are often embalmed in non-Orthodox funeral homes.

5. Does Orthodox Judaism also prohibit cremation?

Yes, and for many of the same reasons as Orthodoxy frowns upon autopsy and embalming.

Cremation was a common pagan custom, and it may indeed be that the leaders of the Jewish community determined that this ban was one way in which Jews should set themselves apart from other people.

In Judaism, it is a *mitzvah* to bury the dead. The Book of Deuteronomy 21:23 clearly states that even the body of a criminal who has been impaled on a stake must be buried. The Talmud goes so far as to say that cremation does not fulfill the *mitzvah* and thus is forbidden.

Cremation was also considered *nivul hamet*. More importantly, cremation effectively precludes decomposition—and thus resurrection and atonement for sins in the eyes of Orthodoxy. Interestingly, the Talmud specifically notes (*Gittin* 56b) that Titus was cremated and underscores this event by relating his instructions: "Burn me and scatter my ashes over the seven seas so that the God of the Jews should not find me and bring me to trial."

Reform Judaism is somewhat more liberal in its view of cremation. While the practice is certainly not encouraged, most Reform rabbis and some Conservative rabbis are sensitive to the wishes of those who have chosen this course.

Preparing for the Funeral Service, Part One

We have already described Orthodox and Liberal practices for caring for the body of the deceased, beginning at the moment of death. But even as the body is being cleansed and prepared for burial, whether by the *chevrah kaddisha* or the funeral home, arrangements for the funeral service itself are also being finalized.

1. How soon after death should the funeral service be held?

Jewish custom dictates that burial should take place as soon as possible, ideally within twenty-four hours after death. This practice originated in biblical times, primarily for reasons of health. The warm Middle-Eastern climate resulted in the immediate onset of decomposition, a condition fostering disease.

By the rabbinic period, certain circumstances were recognized as legitimate causes for delay:

a. The funeral could be postponed so that it would not take place on Shabbat, Yom Kippur, or the first or last day of a Jewish festival.

b. Postponement could occur in order to allow family and friends in distant locales to arrive and attend the funeral.

c. Delay was permitted, if required, to secure a suitable burial place.

Reform Jews do not insist upon burial within twenty-four hours but do hold the service as soon as possible, sensitive to the anguish that families endure in anticipation of a final farewell to their loved ones.

2. Did Jews always use coffins?

No. In ancient Palestine, the dead were most often wrapped in cloth and placed into niches of caves with no distinctive burial ceremony. Genesis 23, for example, describes the Cave of Machpelah, which Abraham purchased as a burial place for his wife, Sarah, and which ultimately became his final resting place as well. The widespread practice of securing family caves and sepulchers helps to explain the biblical statement that, when one dies, one is "gathered to his fathers" (e.g., Judges 2:10). A notable exception to this general practice was the burial of Joseph, as recorded in Genesis 50:26. Joseph was interred in a coffin, but in accordance with Egyptian rather than Jewish custom.

One obvious reason for no coffins was the belief that the speedier the decomposition of the body, the sooner atonement for sins could be completed. The custom of burying the dead without a casket continues in the State of Israel today, where the deceased is lowered into the ground on a bed of reeds.

3. When did coffins become part of Jewish custom?

Use of the casket dates from the period of the Babylonian Exile, when the buried corpse was surrounded by loose boards. This was not a universal practice. Reference to caves, tombs, and catacombs as burial places is also found in the literature of this period. And, indeed, the crypts of great scholars and communal leaders of Palestine can be visited in Israel today.

By about the seventeenth century, Eastern-European Jews had complete, solid caskets for all the people.

4. Are all Jewish coffins the same?

Orthodoxy prescribes the use of a plain wooden box as a casket. It was the great Jewish scholar Maimonides who first promulgated this ruling, both to guard against ostentation and to symbolize that all people are equal in death. Over time, Orthodox practice barred the use of nails or metal in the coffin's construction. Reform Jews use wooden or metal caskets in accordance with the wishes of the family.

5. Why are the Orthodox so adamant in their insistence on a plain wood box?

Genesis 3:19 proclaims: "For dust you are and to dust you shall return." Again we see the Jewish emphasis on bodily remains returning to the earth. This, coupled with the association of decomposition and atonement for sin, led the Orthodox to frown upon any impediment to that end. Since metal does not easily decompose, its use was forbid-

den. The great Jewish scholar Judah Ha-Nasi even instructed his students to bore holes in his coffin in order to hasten the process. Today, some Jews choose a metal casket but have holes drilled in the metal.

6. How is the deceased to be dressed?

From about the second century to the present, following a ruling of Rabban Gamaliel, Orthodox Jews have been buried in simple white shrouds (*tachrichim*), symbolic of the equality of all men and women in death. Also, men are buried wearing a *kipah* and with their *talit* about their shoulders. However, one of the *tzitzit* is cut off to render it *pasul* (ritually unfit).

7. Why are the tzitzit removed?

The *tzitzit* of the *talit* represent the 613 *mitzvot* which are incumbent upon Orthodox Jews. The Hebrew word *tzitzit* has a numerical equivalent of 600. There are eight fringes on the *talit*, with five knots in each, hence a total of 600 + 8 + 5 or 613. The *tzitzit* are cut in recognition of the fact that the dead are no longer responsible for the performance of the *mitzvot*.

8. Are Reform Jews buried in shrouds?

Only in the rarest of circumstances. Reform

Mount of Olives, Jerusalem.

and some Conservative Jews are buried in a suit or a dress, with men sometimes also wearing a *kipah* and/or *talit*.

9. Are there any variations in these customs?

Yes. Some Orthodox men are buried in a *kittel*, a shroud-like garment which they wore on their wedding day, at the Passover seder, and on Yom Kippur.

It is customary for Yemenite men to be garbed in their best clothes under the *tachrichim* since Yemenite culture holds that they are going to meet the Messiah after death. Often, rose water and fragrant leaves are sprinkled upon or placed in the clothing for the same reason.

In some Jewish communities, bits of pottery or coins are placed over the eyes of the deceased. This practice derives from a superstitious belief that only by covering the eyes can our loved ones find true peace, freed from searching and thus from envy and temptation.

10. Why do many Jews have a bag of earth from Israel placed under their heads in the casket?

This practice, not followed by most Reform Jews, is derived from the Orthodox belief in bodily resurrection (in Hebrew, *techiyat hametim*). According to this belief, all Jews will be resurrected in Israel when the Messiah arrives. This will enable the final great judgment on Jerusalem's Mount of Olives. (For this reason, the greatest wish of many Jews is to be buried on the Mount of Olives and thus be among the first to meet the Messiah.)

This notion led to deep concern in the minds of those pious Jews who did not live in Palestine. They wondered: "If I will be buried in a place distant from Palestine, how can I be resurrected in the Holy Land?"

In response to this question, the rabbis advanced the notion of *gilgul hanefesh* (literally, "rolling of the soul"). This legend held that beneath the earth lay a vast system of interconnecting tunnels, ultimately leading to Jerusalem. When the Messiah comes, asserted the legend, all Jewish souls will roll through the tunnels to Jerusalem and resurrection. Those buried in distant lands had only to have a small bag of earth from Israel placed beneath the head in the coffin as a sort of infallible homing device.

While this notion may seem less than credible to the modern mind, it gave many Jews a sense of peace in their final moments on earth, assured of their place in the world to come.

Preparing for the Funeral Service, Part Two

1. Where should the funeral service be held?

Modern Jews generally arrange for a service at a funeral chapel or in the cemetery at graveside. In times past, the service was most often held in a home or, in the case of a great scholar or community leader, within the synagogue building. This latter custom of a temple funeral is still occasionally observed today, both for communal figures and for others who specifically request this setting.

2. Should the body lie in state?

Orthodoxy is very clear in rejecting this practice. The Talmud specifically states: "Do not look upon the face of the dead." Most scholars agree that this prohibition was a rejection of a common Christian custom. Still, there are some Jews who choose to allow friends and family to view the deceased prior to the funeral service. In almost no circumstances, however, does the casket remain open during the service itself.

3. What about music and flowers?

Traditional Judaism discourages instrumental music and flowers at funerals. The chanting or recitation of psalms and prayers is, of course, part of the service. But music per se, considered a form of entertainment, is not permitted. Flowers were frowned upon because the rabbis did not wish to promote ostentation. The rabbinic position on flowers paralleled that of ordaining plain "wood" caskets and simple shrouds. But additionally, Jews were—and are—encouraged to help the living. Thus, beginning in the Middle Ages, in place of flowers, most Jews gave *tzedakah,* a donation to a cause favored by the deceased.

It is important to note that the stances on music and flowers are *minhagim* (customs) which acquired the force of *halachah* (law). Accordingly, many Liberal Jews opt for one or both as personal expressions of their affection and respect for their loved ones. This is especially so with flowers at the grave, a clear expression of *kevod hamet,* "honor for the dead."

4. Does Jewish tradition permit pallbearers?

Yes. Indeed, a Jewish funeral is called a *levayah,* an "accompanying" of the body to the grave. Pallbearers, or "honorary" pallbearers, generally either carry the casket or walk beside the coffin from the chapel to the hearse and, at times, also from the hearse to the grave itself.

5. Who is allowed to serve as a pallbearer?

Members of the family or close Jewish friends usually are asked. It is considered a great *mitzvah* to serve as a pallbearer.

For Liberal Jews, great honor is accorded to the deceased when his or her children or grandchildren are pallbearers. This derives from an account in Genesis 50:13 which relates that [Jacob's] "sons carried him into the land of Canaan." Orthodoxy, however, prohibits this practice.

6. Are women permitted to be pallbearers?

Orthodoxy does not allow women to be pallbearers. This decision was originally made out of concern for the close physical contact between men and women that could occur when dozens of mourners surrounded the casket. Accordingly, women walked either in front of or behind the body of mourners. In fact, there were at one time professional women mourners who were engaged to lead the casket in the funeral procession.

In Reform Judaism, no such prohibition exists, and both women and men share this *mitzvah.*

7. Are funeral services required for infants?

Though the horror of the death of a baby is an event that no one wishes to contemplate, our Jewish tradition faces this tragedy and responds to it.

In Jewish law, a baby that dies within thirty days is considered an aborted child. Therefore, if a baby dies before that time, a formal funeral is not required and the family is released from the obligations of a formal mourning period, including *Kaddish.* If the child dies after thirty days, he or she receives a regular funeral, and the formal mourning procedures are observed.

In Reform Judaism, most parents who have suffered this terrible loss request a graveside service. It is a situation that modern medicine will, God-willing, one day make a faded historical memory.

8. What if the deceased committed suicide?

In Jewish law, suicide is forbidden. A suicide is referred to as *hame'abed atzmo lada'at,* "one who loses himself in knowledge."

Among Jews who strictly follow the letter of the law, those who commit suicide are denied a full funeral service and full mourning and may not be buried in the consecrated portion of a Jewish cemetery. Instead, they are buried outside of this area, at least six feet from other graves.

In recent times, however, Reform and other more liberal Jews, including some Orthodox, have determined that any suicide is the result of illness. That being the assumption, those who take their lives are given a full funeral service and are buried within the cemetery. This sense of compassion for the grief-stricken family, this ability to continually reinterpret Jewish law in light of new knowledge and new insights, is part of what makes our Judaism a living tradition.

The Funeral Service

In contrast to some of the more intricate mourning customs we have studied, the Jewish funeral service is a relatively simple ritual, consisting of the following elements: "cutting *keriah*" prior to the service; recitation of psalms; the *hesped* or eulogy; chanting of the *El Male Rachamim*; and recitation of the mourner's *Kaddish* after interment.

1. Were Jewish funerals always like this?

No. In ancient times, the funeral service began in the home of the deceased. Psalms were recited, followed by a procession past the home to the grave, where the burial took place. There was neither *Kaddish* nor *El Male Rachamim*, both of which originated in later times.

2. What about today?

The major portion of most Jewish funeral services takes place in a funeral chapel or synagogue. A procession then travels to the cemetery, where *Kaddish* is recited following interment.

Some Jews, however, hold the complete service at graveside.

3. How do we "cut keriah"?

As we have already learned, the ritual of *keriah* may take place following the moment of death. More commonly, however, it is observed just prior to the service with only the immediate family present.

To review: In Orthodoxy, only one's actual clothes may be used, a coat or dress. The tear in the garment is never resewn completely. Liberal Jews will often use a black ribbon provided by the funeral home in place of clothing.

Keriah is always performed standing. A cut is made on the left side for parents and on the right side for all others. As the cutting of *keriah* takes place, the family recites the following *berachah*: *Baruch Atah Adonai Elohenu Melech ha'olam Dayan ha'emet.* "Blessed are You, O God, Ruler of the universe, the true Judge." The torn garment is traditionally worn for at least seven days, and often for thirty days, following the funeral.

4. What happens next?

After *keriah*, the service begins. Depending upon local custom, the family either remains in a private room or is seated in the first row of the chapel or synagogue. The closed casket remains in view.

Generally, just prior to the start of the service, the funeral director, rabbi, or a family representative announces where the family will be sitting *shivah*, a seven-day mourning period.

5. How does the actual ceremony begin?

In the Orthodox tradition, the rabbi or the cantor, if one is present, reads or chants one or more psalms, usually Psalms 49, 90, and 91.

6. Why these particular psalms?

Nothing in Jewish law specifically dictates these three psalms, but Orthodox Jewish texts "recommend" them consistently.

The most probable explanation is that the people themselves "chose" these psalms for use at funerals with such regularity that they became an established custom over time.

7. What about Psalm 23, "The Lord Is My Shepherd"?

Inclusion of this psalm in the funeral service was a Reform innovation. Just as Jews of the past were deeply moved by certain of these poetic compositions, so the rabbis and congregants of Reform temples were touched and comforted in grief by Psalm 23 and thus made it their own. Many traditional Jews today have also adopted this psalm as part of the funeral service.

8. What is the hesped or eulogy?

The Hebrew word *hesped* means "mourning," while the Greek-derived "eulogy" means "praise." Both refer to a tribute to the deceased, delivered during the funeral service.

The *hesped* is an old and venerated Jewish custom, dating as far back as at least talmudic times. Its purpose is threefold:

  a. To capture briefly, in an uplifting manner, the life and major accomplishments of the deceased.

b. To pay honor in this manner to the memory of the deceased.

c. To bring comfort to the family and friends who are present.

9. Who delivers the hesped?

The eulogy is usually offered by the rabbi, who spends time with the family prior to the service and becomes acquainted with the life of the deceased through the eyes of those who knew and loved him or her best.

Most rabbis feel that their task is to say what the members of the family would say were they speaking. Accordingly, a eulogy will often contain anecdotes, reminiscences, and occasionally even humorous recollections shared by the family.

10. May anyone other than the rabbi give the eulogy?

Yes. It is not uncommon today for a member of the family to speak instead of or in addition to the rabbi. This tribute may be a speech, a poem, or a reading of something written by the deceased.

The great Jewish poet Chaim Nachman Bialik, for example, wrote a poem entitled "When I Am Dead":

When I am dead, thus shall you mourn me;
There was a man, and see he is no more;
Before his time has come, did this man die;
And his life's song was hushed before it ended.
And woe, and woe, yet one more song,
One more song he had within him,
And lost forever is that song unsung.
Forever lost, forever lost.

11. Are there any times when a hesped may not be offered?

According to Orthodox law, eulogies are not to be part of the funeral service during the month of Nisan and during the holidays of Pesach and Sukot, inasmuch as these seasons of the year celebrate God's great blessing of the Jewish people and are therefore times of great joy.

In Reform Judaism, however, eulogies are considered appropriate at any time. One great Jewish scholar, Rabbi Solomon Freehof, has written that a hesped may be delivered even on Shabbat (though funerals may not take place), if it is edifying and not sad.

12. What is the El Male Rachamim?

El Male Rachamim means "God, full of compassion" and refers to a prayer offered at the conclusion of the service at a chapel or synagogue, and/ or just before the Kaddish if the funeral is held at graveside. The prayer beseeches God to give rest to the soul of the deceased and includes the deceased's Hebrew name.

The El Male Rachamim is a late addition to the funeral liturgy. Though no one knows for certain when it was written, it is usually traced to the seventeenth century, and it has become a standard part of all Jewish funeral services.

13. Why is the Kaddish not part of a chapel or synagogue service?

Jewish law dictates that the Kaddish is to be recited at graveside, just after the casket is covered. When the entire service is at the cemetery, the Kaddish follows the El Male Rachamim. When the service is conducted at a funeral home, the funeral cortege proceeds to the cemetery for Kaddish and other elements of the service.

14. Is a minyan required for a funeral?

In Orthodoxy, a minyan of ten male Jews is required for Kaddish. Technically speaking, a minyan is not required for that portion of the ritual conducted at the funeral home. Still, it is desirable. Orthodox Jews will often ask Jews who are present to make up the minyan, even if they are not part of the funeral party. It is considered a mitzvah to serve in this capacity.

Reform Jews desire but do not demand a minyan at the funeral. Where a minyan is sought, men and women count equally.

15. Are children allowed to attend funerals?

Nothing in Jewish law proscribes a child's attendance at a funeral. Accordingly, the decision should be based on the child's maturity and a sense of whether or not the participation will be beneficial to the young person in expressing grief and in honoring the deceased.

At the conclusion of the *El Male Rachamim*, the casket is carried or rolled out the door to a waiting hearse. Those mourners who will accompany the family to the cemetery go to their cars and form a funeral procession. With the hearse and cars of the family in front, the cortege proceeds to the cemetery.

At the Cemetery

Though Reform and Orthodox customs differ, the cemetery ritual is a solemn and somber embodiment of *halachah* (law), *minhag* (custom), and Jewish values.

Orthodox practice dictates the following procedure:

a. The casket is removed from the hearse.
b. The pallbearers, followed by the rabbi, mourners, and family carry the casket, feet first, to the grave, pausing seven times as Psalm 91 is recited.
c. The casket is lowered into the grave.
d. The rabbi recites *Tzidduk Hadin*.
e. The grave is filled in by the mourners, family, and friends.
f. *El Male Rachamim* is chanted or recited.
g. Sometimes Psalm 49 is read.
h. The mourners recite the *Kaddish Le'itchadeta*.
i. Family and friends of the mourners form two lines. As the mourners walk between them, family and friends recite a special expression of consolation.
j. After passing between the two lines, everyone present plucks some grass and tosses it over his or her right shoulder.
k. The family members return to their cars and proceed back to their home.

1. Is there any required number of pallbearers?

No. Though at least six people usually are needed to carry the weight of the casket, there may be more or fewer.

2. Why is the casket carried feet first to the grave?

The casket is carried in this fashion because of a superstitious belief that the soul of the deceased might otherwise be tempted to "look back" to the world of the living rather than being resigned to the grave. So as not to cause the soul greater anguish, it was spared from "seeing" the world from which it was passing.

3. Why do we pause seven times?

There are at least two explanations for this Orthodox custom, which originated about the ninth century.

The first, and most common explanation, is that the seven pauses correspond to the seven references to life as "vanity" in the biblical Book of Ecclesiastes.

Others assert that each of the seven pauses symbolizes one of the seven heavens of mystical lore.

Still others maintain that the practice served to "shake off" evil spirits and thus assure peace to the soul of the deceased. In ancient times, friends would sometimes offer words of tribute to the deceased at each pause. This practice is sometimes followed in modern times as well. Among the Orthodox, the custom of pausing is not observed when certain prayers of supplication to God, called *Tachanun*, are not recited. *Tachanun* is recited each weekday, except on Rosh Chodesh, Lag Ba'omer, during the month of Nisan, and on other special days. Also, on days when *Tachanun* is not recited, certain portions of the burial service are omitted. Reform cemetery ritual may or may not include the seven pauses, depending upon the rabbi and the wishes of the family.

4. Why is Psalm 91 recited?

As we have seen in the past, this psalm appears to have been "chosen" and fixed by the people themselves as a response to the sorrow of loss.

5. Why do Orthodox Jews lower the casket into the grave?

Traditional Judaism developed a system of both honoring the deceased and helping mourners confront and accept the reality and finality of death. The lowering of the casket was seen as an essential, if often painful, part of that process. In Reform Judaism, the casket is often placed on the grave, covered with a green carpet, and lowered only after the family has departed. This modification in Orthodox practice was instituted out of sensitivity to those for whom the casket's lowering might prove severely traumatic.

6. What is the Tzidduk Hadin?

Tzidduk Hadin, "submission to divine judgment," is a formulation that affirms our acceptance of God's judgment and righteousness, seeks God's compassion and mercy, and concludes in part with the words: "The Lord has given, and the Lord has taken away. Blessed be the name of the Lord."

Tzidduk Hadin dates back to the talmudic period and is generally attributed to Rabbi Chanina Ben Teradyon. According to a talmudic account, Rabbi Chanina defied the Roman Emperor Hadrian's ban against study of the Torah. He and his wife were sentenced to death, and his daughter consigned to a brothel. The story relates that, as the three were being led from the court to their fate, they uttered words of faith that were preserved over the centuries in *Tzidduk Hadin.*

If the entire service is held at graveside, the eulogy, or *hesped,* is usually delivered at this time, following *Tzidduk Hadin.*

7. Is there any prescribed way in which the grave is to be filled in?

Orthodoxy holds that filling in the grave constitutes *kevod hamet,* "honor to the dead," and is an act of the highest respect and caring for our loved ones. Just as we do not enter the world alone, so should we not depart from it alone.

In Orthodoxy, the casket is to be covered completely. Members of the family begin, using only the *back* of the shovel so as not to give the impression of wishing to bury the dead in haste.

For the same reason, the shovel is not passed by hand. Instead, as each mourner fills in a bit of earth, he or she places the shovel in the mound of earth next to the grave before another takes hold of it.

In Reform Judaism, the grave is most often not filled in the presence of the family. Commonly, members of the family will place earth, or even a flower, on the green covering of the casket. However, family and friends often stay behind to assist in, or at least to witness, the interment.

8. Is the El Male Rachamim chanted at graveside even if it has already been done at the chapel?

In Orthodoxy, the *El Male Rachamim* is chanted again at graveside even if it was part of a chapel service. In Reform, the *El Male Rachamim* is usually done only once, at the funeral home if there is a chapel service, or at graveside if there is no chapel service.

Following *El Male Rachamim*, Orthodox Jews sometimes recite Psalm 49.

9. What is the Kaddish Le'itchadata?

The *Kaddish Le'itchadata* (literally, "Kaddish of Renewal") is a special *Kaddish* recited by Orthodox Jews only at graveside. Unlike other forms of *Kaddish*, this formulation explicitly mentions death, the belief in physical resurrection, and confidence in the ultimate rebuilding of the Temple in Jerusalem.

Reform Jews recite the *Kaddish* known as the mourner's *Kaddish*, both at graveside and in the synagogue.

10. What is the expression of consolation recited by friends as mourners leave the grave?

The Hebrew is as follows: *Hamakom yenachem etchem betoch she'ar avele Tziyon Virushalayim.* "May God comfort you along with all the mourners of Zion and Jerusalem."

11. Why do mourners pluck grass and drop it over their shoulders?

Most scholars agree that this custom, which is usually not observed by Reform Jews, originated as an expression of faith in ultimate physical resurrection. Just as grass, though plucked from the ground, grows and flourishes again, so, one day, the Orthodox affirm, we and our loved ones will live again.

Another explanation of this custom emphasizes the transient nature of life. Scripture teaches *yamenu ketzel over*, "our days are like a shadow that passes away." Therefore, our last act in leaving the cemetery is to perform an act that reminds us to love and appreciate those dear to us every moment of every day.

The mourners then proceed to their cars and return home. Among the Orthodox, the family is not permitted to visit the graves of other family members on the day of the funeral, for the sake of *kevod hamet*, total honor and respect for the one who has just been interred.

With the funeral and burial completed, a complex interaction of mourning and comfort is now set into motion.

The Kohen and Some General Background

Before beginning our study of the specific laws and customs of mourning in Jewish tradition, we pause to consider the special situation in Orthodoxy in matters of mourning of *kohanim* (literally,

"priests," descendants of Moses' brother Aaron).

You will recall that of the three categories of Jews in ancient times—*kohen*, *levi*, and *Yisrael*—the *kohen* was restricted in many ways, owing to his unique status in the community. For example, he could not marry a divorcée. He could not perform some of his ritual functions without extensive rites of purification. Similarly, the *kohen*, with rare exceptions, was not and is not permitted to come into contact with the dead, lest he be rendered ritually "impure."

Unless the deceased is his parent, child, sibling, or spouse, a *kohen* cannot enter a funeral home, a synagogue, a cemetery, or a house in which there is a corpse. It is for this reason that Orthodox synagogues do not permit a corpse to be brought into the sanctuary. Accordingly, some Orthodox congregations will not engage a rabbi who is a *kohen* since he cannot officiate at funerals. Some Jewish funeral chapels have erected a special porch outside of the chapel structure so that rabbis who are *kohanim* might deliver a eulogy without violating Orthodox law. In such instances, they speak through a microphone so that they can be heard by those inside.

The difficult dilemma of the *kohen* is not a factor in Reform Judaism since the strict rules regarding *kohanim* were set aside almost from Reform's inception. The founders of Reform rejected the notion of distinctions between Jews. In their eyes, no group of Jews was to be considered as "set apart." Still, traditional proscriptions underscore the special status that those of the priestly class once held in the life of the Jewish community.

1. What are the stages of Jewish mourning?
Orthodoxy delineates a series of steps, beginning with the moment of death, as follows:
   a. *Aninut:* from death to burial.
   b. *Sheloshim:* encompassing thirty days from the day of burial, including the first seven days, *shivah.*
   c. The year following death.

   d. *Yahrzeit:* a perpetual remembrance of loved ones in the context of special worship services.

2. What is the meaning of aninut?
Aninut, a Hebrew word meaning "deep sorrow," is a legal category of mourning used to designate the period from death to burial. An individual who has lost a loved one is referred to as an *"onen"* during this time.

3. Are there any special requirements of an onen?
Quite the contrary. Jewish tradition recognizes that the enormous pain and shock of loss must be respected. Accordingly, an *onen* is freed from the responsibility of observing all positive *mitzvot* (except observing the Shabbat), such as reciting the *Shema* or putting on *tefilin.* In addition, even close friends are instructed not to express condolences "when his dead lies before him" (*Pirke Avot* IV:23), but rather to wait until after the interment. That is why it is only as the family *leaves* the cemetery that friends are first allowed by tradition to utter the traditional words of comfort: "May the Lord comfort you among all the other mourners of Zion and Jerusalem."

4. What is avelut?
Avelut, a Hebrew word meaning "lamenting," refers to the mourning period following interment. A mourner during this period is called an *avel.*

Avelut, which follows *aninut,* encompasses the mourning customs of *shivah, sheloshim,* and, when a parent has died, an entire year. As mourners and friends approach the home, *shivah* begins.

Shivah: Some General Background

"One should not grieve excessively for the dead. . . . The rabbis established limits for each stage of grief and we may not increase them: three days for weeping, seven days for lamenting, and thirty days for refraining from the wearing of laundered clothes and cutting hair. No more."
Shulchan Aruch

The psychological brilliance of Judaism is nowhere more apparent than in its carefully ritualized structure for dealing with grief. The open expression of sorrow is permitted, even encouraged. Yet, beginning with the family's arrival at their home after burial, a process is set into motion that leads the bereaved gently but firmly back to life and the world of the living. The first stage in this gradual process of healing is called *shivah*.

1. What is the meaning of shivah?

Shivah is a Hebrew word meaning "seven" and refers to a seven-day period of formalized mourning by the immediate family of the deceased.

2. When did shivah originate?

The Talmud (*Sanhedrin* 108b) holds that the practice originated prior to the Flood, which is described in the story of Noah in Genesis.

The rabbis of the Talmud cite Genesis 7:10 as the earliest instance of *shivah*: "And it came to pass, *after the seven days*, that the waters of the Flood were upon the earth." The seven days, say the rabbis, were a period of mourning for Methuselah, the oldest man who ever lived.

Likewise, the prophet Amos (8:10) states: "And I shall turn your feasts into mourning." Just as feasts lasted seven days, say the rabbis, so the mourning period into which they were transformed was assumed to have been seven days.

Finally, in Genesis 50:10, the reference is made even more explicit. The text states: "And he [Joseph] mourned for his father [Jacob] for seven days."

3. When does shivah begin?

Shivah begins immediately after the burial and concludes a short time after the morning service (*Shacharit*) seven days later.

4. Where is shivah observed?

It is customary to observe *shivah* in the home of the deceased. Where this is not possible, *shivah* may be marked in the home of an immediate family member or even a friend. Most importantly, however, the family should be together during this time.

5. For whom is shivah observed?

Jewish law prescribes observance of *shivah* for one's parents, sibling, child, or spouse.

6. How does shivah begin?

Before mourners and friends enter the home, Orthodoxy prescribes that they first wash their hands in a ritualistic manner, using a pitcher of water and a basin outside the front or back door.

7. Why are the hands washed?

This custom originated out of superstition and is generally explained in one of three ways.

In ancient times, when an individual died of mysterious causes, the inhabitants of that city often washed their hands at the cemetery, symbolically affirming that they had not shed innocent blood.

In later times, washing the hands became a ritual designed to wash off evil demons that some believed might have attached themselves at the cemetery.

A third rationale for the practice was to cleanse oneself from the ritual impurity associated with death and the cemetery. It was this same assumed impurity that fostered the prohibitions against *kohanim* coming into contact with the dead in any way.

Reform Jews generally do not wash their hands on returning from the cemetery, though some choose to observe this custom.

8. Why do some Jews enter the house of mourning through the back door?

This practice, extremely rare today, derives from a superstitious notion that one should take a different route home from the cemetery than that taken in traveling to it.

9. What happens next?

Upon entering the house, a member of the family generally lights a *shivah* candle, which is almost always provided by the funeral home and which burns for seven days.

10. When did the shivah candle originate?

As far back as the Talmud, Rabbi Judah Ha-Nasi asked his students to keep a light burning after his death, though not specifically as a memorial. Subsequent collections of laws do not refer to the practice, and it is not until at least the thirteenth century that we find evidence of any standardized custom.

While many scholars feel that the custom originated in the thirteenth century, others hold that it emerged from the Italian kabbalists in the seventeenth century. Regardless of its actual beginnings, however, it is clear that the candle was intended to symbolize both the soul of the deceased and the *Shechinah*, the light of God's presence. Scholars, in discussing the matter, often cite Proverbs 20:27: "The light of the Lord is the soul of man."

11. What is the purpose of the shivah candle?

The *shivah* candle, also called the *ner daluk*, "burning light," serves as a mark of respect to the memory of the deceased. In addition, however, there were a host of assumptions based in superstition that came to surround this simple candle.

Jews came to believe that the candle helped the soul ascend to heaven. Some even placed a towel and a glass of water next to the candle so that the soul could take a bath. Still others saw the towel and water as a means of ridding the home of the angel of death. Presumably, the angel of death washed and wiped his sword with these implements, then left, sparing any further tragedy. This latter practice proved distasteful to many Jews and was condemned in the nineteenth century. It has all but disappeared today.

As friends enter the house of mourning, they often find that it looks quite different from its ordinary appearance. That is because Jewish law dictates specific alterations as part of *shivah*.

Shivah: The Home and the Meal of Consolation

1. Does Jewish tradition prescribe any physical changes in the house of mourning?

Yes. There are two customs in particular that bear examination:
   a. Boxes or low stools in place of, or in addition to, chairs.
   b. The covering of all mirrors.

2. What is the purpose of low stools?

It is customary for members of the immediate family to sit on low stools or boxes during the *shivah* period. Indeed, it is probable that this practice resulted in the expression "sitting" *shivah*.

No one knows exactly how the custom originated. Most scholars cite Job 2:13, which, in relating the arrival of Job's three friends to comfort him, says: "For seven days and seven nights they sat beside him on the ground."

Others trace it to II Samuel 13:31, where King David is described as tearing his garments and laying himself on the ground in grief.

Still others hold that we sit on stools to be closer to the ground and thus, symbolically, to our loved ones.

Whatever the exact beginnings of the custom, it became almost universally accepted by Orthodox Jews as a means of expressing grief and as a way of clearly distinguishing this week of sorrow from everyday life.

3. Why are all mirrors covered?

Though we have noted this custom previously, it bears repeating in the context of the *shivah* period in particular. We recall two superstitious fears:
   a. The soul of a person in the home might be "caught" in the mirror and snatched away by the ghost of the deceased.
   b. Due to the supposed presence of the angel of death, those seeing their reflections might place their own lives in jeopardy.

There is no universal halachic prescription for covering mirrors. Wide acceptance of this custom, therefore, may lie in its sensitivity to a human reality. As we shall see, mourners are not to leave the home during *shivah*. Nor are they to shave, use makeup, or attempt to "look their best." The custom of covering mirrors implicitly conveys to the grief-stricken individual that personal appearance simply does not matter now. In doing so, it tacitly removes any cause for embarrassment that mourners might feel.

While neither sitting on stools nor covering mirrors is central to mourning in Reform Judaism, some Reform Jews choose to include one or both practices in their personal observance.

4. What is the meaning of seudat havra'ah?

Seudat havra'ah is a Hebrew term referring to the first meal served to mourners in the house of mourning upon returning from the cemetery. It is commonly known as the "meal of condolence."

5. When did the seudat havra'ah originate?

The first mention of the *seudat havra'ah* occurs in the Talmud. It directs that the first meal after the burial of a loved one must be provided by friends.

By the time of the *Shulchan Aruch,* Jewish law became even more specific and gave not only the law but a possible rationale for it. A mourner is forbidden to eat his own food for the first meal after returning from the cemetery. Some say that this is because a mourner might refuse to eat and prefer to die instead. The meal prepared by neighbors thus helps the mourner to begin to accept life again.

In more recent times, the *chevrah kaddisha* sometimes prepared the meal as part of its communal service, but friends and relatives generally perform this *mitzvah.*

6. What foods are served at the seudat havra'ah?

The traditional meal of comfort usually includes lentils, hard-boiled eggs, and bread—all foods which in Judaism are associated with life. In addition, any other simple and easily digestible food may be served. It is customary, therefore, to make this a dairy meal.

7. Why do we eat lentils?

No one knows for certain, but many interpretations have been offered. Some say that we eat lentils because they are round, like the endless cycle of life or perhaps the circle of fate.

Others assert that the round shape of the lentil suggests the ultimate promise of physical resurrection.

8. Why do we eat eggs?

Egss are an obvious symbol of life. At the seder table on Pesach, a joyous occasion, they are dipped in salt water to acknowledge that life sometimes brings tears and pain. And, at the *seudat havra'ah,* a time of grief, we eat hard-boiled eggs to affirm hope in the face of death.

9. Why must the eggs be hard-boiled?

As eggs harden the more they are cooked, so we eat hard-boiled eggs to symbolize our determination to be resilient in the face of tragedy.

10. Why do we eat bread?

Bread is the staff of life in Judaism and, indeed, in virtually every major faith. At a time of mourning, it is especially appropriate.

11. Is it permitted to have liquor at the seudat havra'ah?

Yes. In fact, one talmudic passage infers that it is praiseworthy for friends to provide mourners with wine. This teaching is based on Proverbs 31:6–7: "Give strong drink unto him that is ready to perish, and wine unto the bitter in soul; let him drink, and forget his poverty, and remember his trouble no more."

Of course, wine or liquor should be drunk in moderation and should not be used as an attempt to totally avoid the reality of bereavement or feelings of loss. The meal of consolation is a *mitzvah,* not in any way a social event.

12. Are any special berachot recited at the seudat havra'ah?

Yes. There is a special section added to the *Birkat Hamazon,* which asks God's comfort for the mourners.

13. May friends bring food to the house of mourning throughout shivah?

Yes. It is considered an act of great caring to free the family from everyday concerns during *shivah.*

The beginning of *shivah* also offers friends an opportunity to express their sympathy through visits to the home. At the same time, those in mourning initiate a process that will ultimately lead them back to the world. This process involves many customs with a twin rationale: acceptance of death and a determination to return to life.

Shivah: The Condolence Call

1. What is the meaning of nichum avelim?

Nichum avelim is a Hebrew term meaning "comforting mourners," and refers in part to the *mitzvah* of visiting the house of mourning during the *shivah* period.

2. When may we begin to visit mourners?

Before burial, grief is so strong as virtually to preclude consolation by even the most well-meaning friend. Accordingly, the appropriate time for a condolence call begins after interment during the *shivah* week.

3. How did condolence calls originate?

Jewish scholars see the condolence call as an ancient custom. The Talmud (*Sotah* 14a), for example, teaches that consoling mourners was originally an act of God. This tractate cites Genesis 25:11 which states: "After the death of Abraham, God brought blessing to Isaac his son." Thus, states the Talmud, just as Isaac was consoled by God's presence, so we are commanded to bring comfort to loved ones with our presence.

In a similar vein, some scholars trace the origin of the condolence call as a response to Isaiah 40:1: "Comfort ye, comfort ye My people."

Most commentators, however, cite the Book of Job 2:13 as the first instance of a condolence call, when Job's three friends "sat down with him upon the ground . . . for they saw that his grief was very great."

4. What is the purpose of a condolence call?

Most mourners do not leave their homes during *shivah*. It is a time to grieve, to work through pain, and then to take a first step back toward life. The process, however, cannot be undertaken alone. The presence of a support system of friends and family is essential to healing. Your visit helps.

Many people are reluctant to visit a house of mourning. They worry about what they should say or do. But what you say or do is the least significant part of a condolence call. Your *presence* is the greatest gift you can give to the bereaved family.

5. What happens when you arrive?

As you enter the house of mourning, a member or friend of the family may meet you and usher you into the living room. It is customary to wait to speak until after the mourner speaks. But, once you are acknowledged, all you need say is "I'm sorry." That simple phrase, a touch, a hug will mean more to the mourner than you can ever know.

6. What happens then?

Shivah is a time when we reminisce, remember, recapture memories of a loved one. As such, what we usually do during a condolence call is to listen to those memories that the *mourner* wishes to share or to talk about other subjects *initiated by the mourner* which may have nothing to do with his or her loss.

Usually, you need not stay more than thirty to forty-five minutes. During your visit, supporting, listening, and responding to the mourner should be your primary goal.

7. Should we bring a gift or flowers?

No. Except for food, as we have already discussed, it is not customary to bring anything with you to the house of mourning. Again, your presence is the main thing. If you wish to "do something," make a contribution to the deceased's favorite charity or to a synagogue fund established in his or her memory. A particularly meaningful gesture for many Jews is to plant trees in Israel through the Jewish National Fund.

8. What if we cannot be physically present during shivah?

It is proper and comforting to write a card or note if you cannot be present. If you were close to the deceased, mourners would usually also welcome a phone call.

9. Can we visit mourners on Shabbat?

Historically, this question has occasioned much dispute among Jewish scholars. In the Talmud (*Shabbat* 12a), for example, the School of Shammai prohibited visiting mourners on Shabbat, while the School of Hillel permitted it, and the law was established according to the School of Hillel.

Since Jewish law prohibits sitting *shivah* on Shabbat, some scholars have asserted that receiving visitors *could* create the impression that the family was violating *halachah.* Therefore, powerful custom has resulted in the prohibition of Shabbat *shivah* visits, at least among the Orthodox.

10. May we pay more than one condolence call during shivah?

Yes. If you are close to the family, it is appropriate for you to come each day, particularly for the daily *minyan* which is a central custom of *shivah.*

Shivah: Customs and Restrictions

The *shivah* period is divided into two parts:
a. The first three days, considered the period of most intensive mourning.
b. The remaining four days.

1. Why are the first three days considered to be the most intense?

Modern psychology has demonstrated that the first few days after the death of a loved one are a time of shock and disorientation.

Long ago, our Jewish ancestors intuited this same phenomenon without benefit of scientific evidence.

Scholars over the centuries have presented a number of interpretations as to why the period is three days, as opposed to two or four.

One explanation is derived from Genesis 22, the story of the binding of Isaac, which we read on Rosh Hashanah. In this account, you will recall that God instructs Abraham to bring his son Isaac to a particular mountain and offer him there as a sacrifice. The journey to the mountain takes three days. The medieval commentator Rashi asserted that God chose a place that required a three-day journey so that Abraham could have time to think carefully about his decision.

In a like manner, the first three days of *shivah* are a time of reflective contemplation of loss.

Rashi also comments on Genesis 18:1, where God is pictured as appearing to Abraham at Mamre to inquire as to his welfare. When did God come? Three days after Abraham's circumcision, says Rashi, indicating perhaps that God waited a suitable time to allow Abraham's pain to heal.

Finally, in a collection known as *Midrash Rabbah,* the rabbis advance a notion that is obviously rooted in superstition. For three days after death, say the rabbis, the soul of the deceased hovers over the body, waiting to reenter. By the end of the third day, the appearance of the body begins to change, and the soul is forced to accept the fact that it cannot reclaim its physical form. Likewise, it takes at least three days for people to begin to accept the reality of loss.

Whatever the original rationale for marking three days, traditional Jewish mourners (those who have lost a parent, spouse, sibling, or child) almost never leave the house except to attend synagogue on Shabbat.

2. What does tradition forbid during shivah?

Among those things traditional Judaism generally proscribes during *shivah* are:

a. Leaving the house, except to go to synagogue on Shabbat.
b. Work or any business pursuits.
c. Shaving or haircuts.
d. Bathing, other than for the most elementary hygiene.
e. The use of cosmetics.
f. The wearing of leather shoes.
g. Festivities of any kind.
h. The wearing of new clothes.
i. Engaging in sex.
j. Studying the Bible, except for Job and some sections of Jeremiah pertaining to sorrow.

3. Why are we allowed to leave the house on Shabbat?

Jewish tradition forbids mourning on Shabbat and specifies that mourners are to go to the synagogue on the first Shabbat following a loved one's death.

It is customary for friends to refrain from extending casual greetings (e.g., "Shabbat Shalom") at the temple. Instead, as mourners enter the synagogue, traditional Jews say: *Hamakom yenachem etchem betoch she'ar avele Tziyon Virushalayim.* "May God comfort you along with all the mourners of Zion and Jerusalem."

4. Are there any other circumstances under which we may leave the house during shivah?

Yes. Jewish law allows those who would otherwise experience *severe* financial loss to return to work after three days.

In addition, there are certain Jewish holidays whose occurrence terminates *shivah* since the *mitzvah* of participating in them takes precedence over personal grief. The major observances that "break" *shivah* are Pesach, Shavuot, Sukot, Rosh Hashanah, and Yom Kippur. Since the rules can be complicated, it is best to consult your rabbi at the beginning of *shivah* to determine its proper length in your situation.

5. Why are shaving, haircuts, and the use of cosmetics forbidden?

We have already discussed the custom of covering mirrors in the house of mourning as a way of emphasizing that personal appearance is unimportant at a time of grief. The same rationale holds for shaving, haircuts, cosmetics, bathing, and the wearing of new clothes.

6. Why do we refrain from wearing leather shoes?

It is customary to wear slippers or rubber or canvas shoes during *shivah*. Leather shoes are not worn because they are considered a luxury (Talmud, *Yora Deah*), and also as a reflection of mourning customs at the time of the prophet Ezekiel (24:17). In addition, since the wearing of leather shoes is associated with going out of the house, there is no need to wear them during *shivah*.

7. Why do we abstain from sex?

During *shivah*, mourners are to refrain from all pleasurable activities, sex among them. Likewise, traditional Jews will not read books for enjoyment, watch television, listen to the radio, or engage in other similar pursuits.

8. Is this also why we do not read from the Bible?

Yes. Traditional Jews will read only those sections of the Bible which deal with coping with grief, specifically Job and portions of the Book of Jeremiah.

9. Must we wear black during shivah?

No. Wearing black is not required. Dark clothes are not mentioned in the Bible and only alluded to in the Talmud. Though some Jews in Egypt wear black for the entire year following a bereavement, it is not a widespread custom in any other Jewish community.

10. Do Reform Jews observe all of the traditional shivah customs?

While there are some Reform Jews who do follow the letter of Jewish law, this is a matter of personal choice and not obligation.

Almost all Reform Jews sit *shivah* for at least three days, and many sit the entire week.

There are two other customs of *shivah* that bear repeating, one extremely rare, the other quite common.

The first is a practice rooted in superstition that occurs at the end of *shivah*. In some communities, at the conclusion of *shivah*, mourners walk outside of their homes and around the block, ostensibly escorting the soul of the deceased out of the home and allowing it to ascend heavenward at last.

A practice that is far more common, and a requirement of Jewish law, is a service twice each day, morning and evening (except on Shabbat), in the place of *shivah*. This allows the mourners to recite the *Kaddish*, since they are not permitted to leave their homes during this period.

The Kaddish

1. Why is there a daily minyan in the house of mourning?

Jewish law requires mourners to recite the mourner's *Kaddish* three times each day—morning, afternoon, and evening—during *shivah*. Since a *minyan* of ten adult male Jews is required in order to say the mourner's *Kaddish*, and since mourners are not allowed to leave the home except on Shabbat, friends and family come to the home to enable the bereaved to fulfill this *mitzvah*.

Liberal Jews most often have only one *minyan* each day, usually in the late afternoon or early evening. Women and men count equally in the composition of the *minyan*, and *Kaddish* may be recited with less than ten Jews present, though a *minyan* is desirable.

2. What is the meaning of Kaddish?

Kaddish is an Aramaic word meaning "sanctification." It is derived from the Hebrew word *kodesh* ("holy"), which is also the root of the Hebrew words *kiddush* ("blessing over wine") and *Kedushah* ("the sanctification" in the prayer service), and the Aramaic word *kiddushin* ("the wedding service").

3. Why do we call it the mourner's Kaddish? Isn't there only one Kaddish?

No. There are many forms of the *Kaddish*, only one of which is the mourner's *Kaddish*.

4. When did the Kaddish originate?

There are many theories as to the origin of the *Kaddish*. One Jewish legend holds that angels brought it down from heaven as a gift from God.

Some scholars, however, believe that the *Kaddish* was written by Jews during the Babylonian Exile (586–38 B.C.E.) or by rabbis of the first or second centuries C.E.

5. Is the Kaddish written in Hebrew?

No. With the exception of the last paragraph, *Oseh Shalom*, the *Kaddish* is written in Aramaic, the vernacular of Babylonian times, thus lending credence to the theory of its Babylonian origins. The *Oseh Shalom* was a later addition to the *Kaddish* prayer.

6. How was the Kaddish originally used?

In the ancient Babylonian academies, the *Kaddish* was recited at the end of a study session or a learned discourse. Only later was it inserted into the service as a prayer in memory and honor of dead scholars.

Over time, five forms of the *Kaddish* became part of Orthodox liturgy:

a. *Chatzi* ("Half") *Kaddish*
   Recited by the reader at the end of a section of the service.
b. *Kaddish Shalem* ("Full" *Kaddish*)
   A concluding prayer for the end of the service.

Grave of Maimonides at Tiberias.

c. *Kaddish deRabbanan* ("Rabbis" *Kaddish*)
   A concluding prayer after the reading of rabbinic material.
d. *Kaddish Leithchadatha* ("Burial" *Kaddish*)
   Recited at graveside at the cemetery.
e. *Kaddish Yatom* ("Orphan's" *Kaddish*)
   This is the form of *Kaddish* we refer to as the mourner's *Kaddish*.

7. Which forms of the Kaddish specifically mention death?

Only the Orthodox graveside *Kaddish* mentions death. The *Kaddish* is a prayer which praises God, expresses the hope that the messianic kingdom will come soon, and supplicates God to bring peace to the world.

8. How did the Kaddish become a prayer for the dead?

The roots of the association between the *Kaddish* and the dead probably date back to the Talmud. One talmudic passage states that recitation of the *Kaddish* wins forgiveness for sins, while another teaches that reciting *Kaddish* maintains the world.

In other words, the *Kaddish* was seen as pleasing to God.

During this era, the *Kaddish* was inserted into the prayer service, to honor the memory of scholars. In addition, during this same period, Rabbi Akiba was said to have helped redeem a father's soul by teaching the man's son to recite *Kaddish* at services.

Over the next several centuries, belief in the mystical power of the *Kaddish* to redeem the souls of the dead continued to spread. Some scholars hold that this belief was "borrowed" from the German Requiem Mass of the Middle Ages, a service which sought to help souls ascend from purgatory to heaven. In the twelfth and thirteenth centuries, the mourner's *Kaddish* became a formal part of the prayer service. It first appeared in the *Mahzor Vitry* in 1208, then in virtually every subsequent prayer book to this day.

9. How was the Kaddish supposed to redeem the souls of the dead?

The Talmud (Rosh Hashanah 17a) asserts that the souls of the unrighteous were consigned for a maximum of twelve months to a sort of nether-world where they remained until purified sufficiently to return to God. The *Kaddish*, it was believed, speeded this process.

10. For whom is Kaddish recited?

Jewish law requires the recitation of the mourner's *Kaddish* for parents, spouses, siblings, and children. For parents, *Kaddish* is to be recited daily for eleven months following burial. For all other relatives, the *Kaddish* is recited for thirty days, the period known as *sheloshim*.

11. Why eleven months for parents? Shouldn't it be twelve months?

The maximum twelve-month purification process of a soul was only required for individuals who were totally evil. Based on the belief that no child should ever have to acknowledge the possibility of a completely wicked parent, Orthodoxy shortened the required period to eleven months. Reform Jews generally say *Kaddish* for twelve months, retaining the talmudic custom.

12. Who says Kaddish?

Originally, only sons said *Kaddish* for their parents. Since this was such a respected *mitzvah*, parents would often refer to their sons as "my *Kaddish*." When there was no son, a family would often hire someone to say *Kaddish* during the eleven-month period.

13. What about daughters?

In Orthodoxy, women are not required to recite *Kaddish*, and are sometimes discouraged from doing so.

There is a powerful story told of Henrietta Szold. When her mother died, a male friend offered to recite *Kaddish* for her mother in her stead. Szold wrote a letter to her friend, which read in part:

"It is impossible for me to find words in which to tell you how deeply I was touched by your offer to act as *Kaddish* for my dear mother. . . . You will wonder, then, why I cannot accept your offer. . . . The *Kaddish* means to me, that the survivor publicly and markedly manifests his wish and intention to assume the relation to the Jewish community which his parent had, so that the chain of tradition remains unbroken from generation to generation. . . . I believe that the elimination of women from such duties was never intended by our law and custom; women were freed from positive duties when they could not perform them, but not when they could. . . . My mother had eight daughters and no son, yet never did I hear a word of regret pass the lips of either my mother or my father that one of us was not a son. When my father died, my mother would not permit others to take her daughters' place in saying the *Kaddish*, and so I am sure I am acting in her spirit when I am moved to decline your offer. . . ."

In Reform Judaism, both men and women may and should recite *Kaddish* for a deceased parent.

14. Why do we stand during the Kaddish?

In Orthodox congregations, only mourners stand during the mourner's *Kaddish*, as a way of alerting the community to those in grief and perhaps in need of an extra measure of caring. In Reform congregations, the entire congregation rises, as a symbol of respect to the memory of the departed, to recite *Kaddish* for those who have no one to say it for them, and for victims of the Holocaust.

Sheloshim and the Year of Mourning

1. What is the meaning of sheloshim?

Sheloshim is a Hebrew word meaning "thirty" and refers to the traditional thirty-day period of mourning following burial.

2. When did sheloshim originate?

Jewish tradition holds that *sheloshim* originated in biblical times. The Book of Deuteronomy 34:8 states that the Israelites mourned the death of Moses for thirty days. Earlier in Deuteronomy (21:13), a woman taken captive in battle is commanded to mourn her parents' death for a full month.

By the time of the Mishnah, *sheloshim* had apparently become an accepted custom. In fact, Judah Ha-Nasi, the great codifier of Jewish law, expressed a last wish that his school be reopened thirty days after his impending death.

3. How does sheloshim differ from shivah?

Sheloshim includes the seven days of *shivah*. However, the twenty-three days following the conclusion of *shivah* are far less restrictive.

4. May sheloshim be shortened by a Jewish festival?

Yes. Even as Pesach, Shavuot, Sukot, Rosh Hashanah, and Yom Kippur curtail *shivah*, so do they "break" *sheloshim*, except in the case of a parent. Your rabbi can advise you as to your individual circumstances.

5. What are the traditional rules of sheloshim?

After *shivah* ends, mourners may return to work. The rules for the balance of *sheloshim*, however, wisely prescribe that they not immediately resume a normal daily routine. Specifically:

a. Mourners continue to recite *Kaddish* in the presence of a *minyan* three times daily. This provision requires attendance at daily services, and also insures that the bereaved will be regularly in the midst of a sympathetic support group.

b. Mourners do not attend parties or other festive occasions, especially if there is to be music and/or dancing. If a previously planned extended-family *simchah* falls within *sheloshim*, a wedding or *bar mitzvah*, for example, mourners may attend the religious service but not the party. If a religious *simchah* in the immediate family occurs during *sheloshim*, it should not be postponed, but any music should be cancelled.

c. Mourners do not watch television, listen to the radio, or go to movies, sporting events, or purely social gatherings. As these are forms of entertainment, they are prohibited during *sheloshim*.

d. Mourners do not visit the graves of their loved ones. Custom, not *halachah*, prescribes that the grave not be visited for the duration of *sheloshim*. Reform Jews, however, feel free to visit the cemetery after the end of *shivah*.

6. How does sheloshim conclude?

It has become customary to hold a brief memorial service on the morning of the thirtieth day, particularly if the deceased was a Jewish leader or scholar. This is not a second funeral but, rather, a way to formally mark the end of another stage in the mourning process and a continuation of reentry to daily life.

In the course of the service, a rabbi, family member, or friend may say a few words about the deceased, and *Kaddish* is recited.

7. Do Reform Jews observe sheloshim?

Though *sheloshim* is not as deeply rooted in Reform as it is in Orthodoxy, many Reform Jews choose to embrace the spirit, if not all of the specifics, of *sheloshim*. Most Reform Jews recite *Kaddish*, whether daily at a temple *minyan* or weekly at Shabbat services. Many choose to avoid parties and social occasions. Generally, a memorial service is held after the thirty days. Experience has taught us that *sheloshim* can be a precious period of healing and thus meaningful in our lives.

8. What happens after sheloshim?

Sheloshim concludes the traditional mourning period for all loved ones, except for parents. Most mourners may return to a full business and social life.

9. What if we are mourning parents?

As we have seen, Orthodox Jews formally mourn the loss of parents for eleven months, Reform Jews for twelve.

Reform Jews may recite *Kaddish* at a daily *minyan* or regularly at Shabbat services. The restrictions on social activities are a matter of personal choice.

The Tombstone

As the year of mourning moves toward completion, the family should begin to make plans for the setting of a headstone at the gravesite of their loved one.

1. Did Jews always have tombstones?

No. In biblical times, most Jews were buried in simple, unmarked graves, in open fields, or in family caves. Some families had sufficient means and stability such that generations of their members were all buried in a single cave. Hence the biblical phrase: "And he was gathered to his fathers."

2. Are tombstones mentioned in the Bible?

Yes. In the Book of Genesis 35:20, Jacob is described as setting up a pillar at the site of his wife Rachel's grave. To this day, tourists to Israel visit "Rachel's Tomb." In II Kings 23:17–18, King Josiah sees the tomb of a prophet and instructs that it not be disturbed. Finally, the prophet Ezekiel (39:15) commands that, if the bones of the dead are found, "set up a sign by it." Thus we see that, while headstones were not the norm among the Israelites, they were not unknown.

3. How did Judaism come to adopt the use of tombstones?

Most scholars assert that Jews began to use tombstones as a result of the influence of the Greeks and the Romans. The Mishnah refers to a set time each year, the first day of the month of Adar, when all grave sites were marked with a sort of white plaster, and often a small pile of stones. This served to guard against the inadvertent desecration of these final resting places, and enabled *kohanim* to keep the required distance from forbidden graves.

The tomb of Herzl. Lower right: commemorative stamp issued in his honor.

Later in this period, the use of tombstones, grave markers, and occasionally even elaborate monuments became prevalent.

4. What is the Hebrew word for tombstone?

At least two terms were used to designate the various types of grave markers:

a. *Matzevah* ("Monument")
   The sort of marker that Jacob erected for Rachel.
b. *Tziyun* ("Signpost")
   A simple marker, usually used to mark the graves of *kohanim*.

It is fitting that modern Jews use the word *matzevah* to designate the stone we select for those we loved so dearly, even as Jacob crafted one for his beloved Rachel.

5. When did the use of tombstones become widespread?

By the fifth or sixth century, most Jews had tombstones, and, eleven centuries later, by the time of the *Shulchan Aruch*, the custom had become law. A monument of some kind was seen as a means of honoring the dead, of marking the grave for "all time" so that the name of the individual would not be forgotten, and, among the superstitious in the Middle Ages, as a way of preventing the ghost of the person from escaping.

6. What did Jews inscribe on tombstones?

At first, nothing. As with the use of monuments, the notion of inscriptions was borrowed from the Greeks and Romans.

Over time, certain elements became standard for all markers:

a. The full Hebrew name of the deceased.
b. The Hebrew calendar date of death.
c. The English (or French or Turkish) name.
d. The secular calendar dates of birth and death.

In addition, some Jews began to add symbols and Hebrew phrases to the stones of their beloved.

7. What were the most common symbols?

The most frequently employed symbols then, as today, include:

a. The seven-branched menorah
   Symbol of the Israelites in the Bible and of the State of Israel today.
b. Hands raised in blessing (for *kohanim*)
   This symbol, the hands of the *kohanim*, reflects the hope that God will grant the deceased the peace mentioned in the threefold priestly benediction.
c. A cup
   Symbolically, the cup of the Levites in the Jerusalem Temple, common for Jews who are *levi*.

From time to time, particularly ornate Jewish tombstones display a photograph of the deceased mounted in heavy plastic, but this is very rare.

8. What were the most common phrases?

It would be more accurate to refer to them as inscriptions rather than phrases. Often, a mother's stone would include a section from Proverbs 31 ("A woman of valor"). It was quite common for a stone to carry the Hebrew letters representing the Hebrew phrase meaning "May his (her) soul be bound up in eternal life."

9. How do we select monuments today?

Arrangements for a gravestone should be made as soon as possible after the funeral. The size of the stone and the inscription should be a family decision. Your local funeral director can recommend one or more stonesmiths. The monument may be made out of stone or metal, upright or flat. It should be dignified and not ostentatious. Your rabbi can help you select an appropriate text, which should be reviewed carefully *before* the stone is prepared.

10. Does Judaism permit mausoleums or crypts?

Jewish tradition prefers that these forms of monuments not be used, inasmuch as they do not afford the body a return to the earth. Some Jews, however, have chosen to be so interred.

When the stone is ready, it is set at the head of the grave, then covered with a veil or thin cloth in preparation for a ceremony called the unveiling.

The Unveiling

1. What is an unveiling?

An unveiling is a graveside religious ceremony marking the formal setting of a loved one's headstone at the cemetery.

2. Is the unveiling ceremony biblically based?

No. The unveiling has no Jewish historical roots. It is an American custom, recent in origin, borrowed and adapted from American culture.

3. When is the unveiling held?

In Orthodoxy, the stone is not set until after the conclusion of twelve months. Most Jews, therefore, hold the unveiling service at the end of the year of mourning.

4. What if the end of "the year" falls during winter months?

It is not at all uncommon to change the unveiling to a more convenient time, so long as it is after the conclusion of the year's mourning period. A date change may be occasioned by considerations of weather or the inability of family members to attend on a particular date.

5. Is there a prescribed ritual for an unveiling?

No. Custom dictates a brief ceremony, with immediate family and perhaps a few very close friends present. Generally, psalms are recited, followed by some brief words about the deceased, the actual unveiling of the stone, the *El Maley Rachamim*, and the *Kaddish*. Orthodoxy requires a *minyan* for *Kaddish*, while Reform does not.

An unveiling should not be a second funeral. Most Jews choose to ask their rabbi to conduct the service, but the presence of a rabbi or cantor is not required. An unveiling is intended as a family tribute to the memory of a loved one, a private, tender time of reminiscence after "the year" of mourning comes to an end. We perform the *mitzvah* of *kever avot* (literally, "grave of the fathers") by visiting the grave, and leave the ceme-

tery with a greater sense of closure and a renewed commitment to life.

6. Why do some people leave pebbles on the headstone as they leave the cemetery?

In biblical times, as we have seen, graves were sometimes marked by a pile of stones. Some scholars suggest that this may explain the custom of leaving pebbles. There is no religious basis for the practice. It serves to indicate that loved ones have been to the grave, and that alone is sufficient cause to justify it. At least one contemporary rabbi, however, has suggested that leaving a stone may also have therapeutic benefit for us, especially if we see it as a symbolic means of leaving behind some of the "hardness" of grief and pain.

7. Is there a meal in the home following the unveiling?

There is no requirement for the equivalent of the "meal of consolation" that follows a funeral. Some Sephardic Jews bring food to the cemetery itself. If Ashkenazic Jews do invite family members to the home following the service, it is a gesture of graciousness rather than a religious obligation.

8. How often should we visit the grave after "the year" concludes?

There is no prescribed minimum or maximum number of visits. Orthodox Jews make a point of visiting the graves of loved ones during the month of Elul just prior to the onset of the High Holy Days, on the day before Rosh Hashanah, and the day before Yom Kippur. Many Jews visit the cemetery on the loved one's birthday, an anniversary, or a special personal day. Visitations to the cemetery are not made on Shabbat or Jewish festivals.

Jewish tradition discourages excessive mourning and constant cemetery visitation, especially if it becomes an impediment to a return to life. The Book of Jeremiah 22:10 proclaims: "Weep ye not (too much) for the dead." Wisely, though, Jewish practice provides for a regular, structured, communal expression of reminiscence, through *Yahrzeit* and *Yizkor*.

Yahrzeit and Yizkor

1. What is the meaning of Yahrzeit?

Yahrzeit is a German/Yiddish word meaning "year's time" and refers to the annual Jewish commemoration of a loved one's death.

2. How did the observance of Yahrzeit originate?

The custom of marking the anniversary of a loved one's passing is very old in Judaism. The Talmud mentions a son who fasted on the anniversary of his father's death. We also know that students of great talmudic scholars marked the anniversaries of their teachers' deaths by visiting their gravesites.

Most scholars agree that the *Yahrzeit* commemoration as we know it today arose between the fourteenth and seventeenth centuries in Germany. Its essence was borrowed from the Christian church practice of honoring the dead at annual masses and lighting candles in their memory.

3. How is the date of Yahrzeit fixed?

Traditional Jews mark the Hebrew calendar anniversary of death, while most Reform Jews observe the secular calendar date.

4. What are the religious practices associated with Yahrzeit?

Yahrzeit is generally a personal, rather than a communal, observance. Though the *Yahrzeit* of a great Jewish leader may be marked communally, it is the individual family member who most often takes sole responsibility for assuring that a loved one is remembered.

Orthodoxy prescribes the following practices:

a. Lighting a 24-hour *Yahrzeit* candle on the eve of the anniversary. *Yahrzeit* candles are available in many grocery stores.

b. For sons, recitation of *Kaddish* for parents at services on the *Yahrzeit* date. Some sons will conduct services in memory of a parent and often are called to the Torah for an *aliyah,* to recite the *berachot* before and after the Torah reading.

c. Illumination of a memorial plaque light in the synagogue which bears the name of the deceased.

d. Visiting the cemetery.

e. Giving *tzedakah.*

f. Special acts of kindness to others.

g. Study of Torah.

h. Fasting.

Many Reform Jews light *Yahrzeit* candles. Both men and women recite *Kaddish* at temple on the Shabbat closest to the secular calendar anniversary and visit the cemetery close to the *Yahrzeit* date.

5. What is the meaning of Yizkor?

Yizkor is a Hebrew word meaning "remembrance" and refers to special services associated with certain Jewish holidays which are specifically dedicated to the memory of our loved ones.

6. When are Yizkor services held?

In Orthodoxy, *Yizkor* services take place on Yom Kippur, Shemini Atzeret, and on the last days of Pesach and Shavuot.

At one time, Reform congregations had *Yizkor* services only on Yom Kippur and Pesach. Today, growing numbers of Reform temples have added services on Sukot and Shavuot.

7. When did the custom of Yizkor originate?

While there are a few scholars who believe that *Yizkor* began as early as the time of the Maccabees (165 B.C.E.), most historians place the beginnings of *Yizkor* just after the First Christian Crusade of 1096 C.E. In the wake of mass slaughters of entire Jewish communities in Germany during this period, synagogues instituted a memorial service to honor these martyrs. Subsequently, there also arose a prayer for the souls of the dead, which in turn became *Yizkor* as we know it.

Yizkor undoubtedly took shape in part as a borrowing from the Christian All Souls Day and All Saints Day. In time, *Yizkor* became a service during which Jews prayed for both martyrs and their own deceased loved ones. During the eighteenth century, the lone Yom Kippur service was increased to four *Yizkor* services, as it is today.

8. Why do some people leave the sanctuary during Yizkor?

Orthodox Jews leave the synagogue during *Yizkor* if their parents are alive. This practice is based in part upon a superstition that harm might come to their parents if they remained. Reform Jews remain for *Yizkor,* even if their parents are living, and recite *Kaddish* for all the unnamed and nameless who have no children to pray for their eternal rest.

Yizkor and *Yahrzeit* bring the Jewish cycle of mourning to a close. Though our dead are never forgotten, and though we continue to recite *Kaddish* for them so long as we live, we now rejoin life with full vigor.

Conclusion

It is frequently said that the synagogue makes Jews, while other Jewish organizations make use of Jews. That is only partly true. The synagogue has a symbiotic relationship with the home. If the home is Jewishly illiterate and indifferent, the synagogue can labor mightily, but its impact will be diminished.

A vibrant Jewish home is the seed-bed of Jewish culture, identity, and practice. A cardiac Judaism—"I feel it in my heart"—is grossly inadequate. Only a Jewish life which is knowledgeable and rooted in Jewish history and practice can be truly authentic.

It is crucial that we, as Reform Jews, have the background which enables us to choose rites, practices, and ceremonies that are meaningful to us. It is slander to suggest that "it is easy to be a Reform Jew" because no demands are made on us. In truth, it is *hard* to be an authentic Reform Jew. We have to know what Judaism is all about so we can use our best judgement and make our own choices about a Jewish lifestyle congenial to our values.

In helping Reform Jews to make such choices, Rabbi Daniel Syme has made a unique contribution through the "Jewish Home" series. Rabbi Syme credits me with the idea. I am honored; it is one of my better ideas. Rabbi Syme has given us a practical guide on how each of us can own a portion of a faith—modern, yet ancient—whose values resonate through all of human history and can enrich our lives today.

Reform Jews give to *halachah* (Jewish law) a respectful vote but not a veto. Such choices cannot be made by the ill-informed, for Judaism must never be reduced to a religion of convenience. Rabbi Syme has shared with us the Jewish materials we need to choose wisely from the richness of Jewish religious experience.

Albert Vorspan